Images of War

RAF FIGHTER PILOTS OVER BURMA

NORMAN FRANKS

Pen & Sword
AVIATION

First published in Great Britain in 2014 by
PEN & SWORD AVIATION
an imprint of
Pen & Sword Books Ltd,
47 Church Street,
Barnsley,
South Yorkshire.
S70 2AS

A CIP record for this book is available from the British Library.

ISBN 978 1 78337 614 8.

Printed and bound by CPI UK

Pen & Sword Books Ltd incorporates the Imprints of
Pen & Sword Aviation, Pen & Sword Maritime,
Pen & Sword Military, Wharncliffe Local History, Pen & Sword Select,
Pen & Sword Military Classics and Leo Cooper.

For a complete list of Pen & Sword titles please contact
Pen & Sword Books Limited
47 Church Street, Barnsley, South Yorkshire, S70 2AS, England

E-mail: enquiries@pen-and-sword.co.uk
Website: www.pen-and-sword.co.uk

Contents

INTRODUCTION

When the Japanese attacked the American Fleet in Pearl Harbor on 7 December 1941, the war in Europe was two years and three months old. Britain was just about holding its own, having been kicked out of France in May 1940, managed to survive the Battle of Britain and then the RAF had staged something of a comeback over Northern France in 1941, although not without severe losses of fighter pilots and fighter aeroplanes.

Fighting in North Africa had not gone well, with British forces retreating and advancing across the Western Desert in desperate attempts to keep the Axis forces away from the Middle East oilfields. Malta was holding off massive air attack and, like the Desert, was yet another drain on fighter aircraft and personnel. All this time anxious eyes had been looking towards the Far East, wondering if the Japanese Empire would attempt to spread its influence across the Pacific and the South Seas, even into British territory of Malaya and India itself. Burma, too, would be an obvious staging post for an assault on India and, if the Japanese headed south, Australia would also come under threat.

Despite these worries it was obvious that the war in Europe would be using most of the resources available, and even Malta and North Africa would take second place in the pecking order. Some thought had been given to the defence of Britain's major base in the Far East, Singapore, but the handful of RAF and Australian squadrons based there were using a fairly antiquated fighter aeroplane, the American Brewster Buffalo. This stubby little fighter, designed for the US Navy, was more like a flying club machine of the 1930s. It was lightly armed and when examples were bought by the RAF in 1940 it was soon rejected for front-line service in Europe and sent out to Singapore. It would never be able to stand against the German Messerschmitt 109 fighter, but would be better than nothing against Japanese aircraft, none of which were thought to be serious contenders for air superiority. Even Japanese pilots were not deemed well enough trained to oppose British or American aircrew. More derogatory comments from American journalists even suggested Japanese pilots, wearing thick-lensed spectacles, could hardly see to fly! Towards the end of 1941, Curtiss Mohawk fighters, originally meant to be supplied to the French air force, were also sent out to the Far East, but they too were found wanting, although some remained active in Burma until the end of 1943.

There were a few operationally experienced fighter pilots available to go to the Far East during 1941, and shortly before the Japanese attacked Pearl Harbor, other units were on their way to North Africa to help support the latest see-sawing battle front. Some of these were quickly diverted to the Far East; it was a slow and meandering journey, but at least these units were either taking or were to be quickly equipped with Hawker Hurricane fighters. However, by the time the first of these reinforcements arrived, Singapore had already fallen, and the reinforcements, such as they were, ended their journey at Rangoon.

Another force in that Singapore region was the American Volunteer Group – the AVG – made up of volunteer (mercenary) airmen from the USA, both former Army and Navy pilots, who saw a chance of action and, hopefully, some monetary reward from the Chinese, who employed them. The Chinese, of course, had been at war with Japanese forces in China for some time. The Americans had Curtiss P-40 Tomahawk fighters, a very reasonable aeroplane, and the same that the RAF was also using in the Western Desert, and to good effect.

Although the AVG was set up before the US came into the war, it did not see any action until after 7 December 1941. By this time the AVG in China had been formed into three squadrons, and within days of Pearl Harbor, one of them, consisting of twenty-one P-40s and twenty-five pilots, was sent to Rangoon's Mingaladon airfield.

The scene was set. The Japanese had been rushing to engage the British at Singapore and, now, Rangoon, to be followed by a planned push north across Burma, along the Bengal coast, or centrally towards Assam. India was the target. All that had stood in their way at Singapore were those few squadrons of antiquated fighters, some Blenheim bombers and a few Westland Lysander army-cooperation aeroplanes. One Japanese ally was the fear-factor. Their brutality in China was becoming well known and however determined the British soldiers were to stem the Japanese advance, they were on the back foot from the start, with poor equipment and with the thought in the back of their minds that to be captured by this ruthless enemy was not to be contemplated.

When the Japanese did strike it was still something of a surprise when Japanese naval air power sank two Royal Navy capital ships with seemingly consummate ease on 10 December 1941 – HM Ships *Prince of Wales* and *Repulse* off the Malayan coast. Fighters had been sent out to assist – 453 Squadron's Buffaloes – but they arrived too late. The plan had been to inform this squadron should the ships leave harbour, but the RAF were not alerted before they sailed. No doubt the Navy felt quite capable of looking after themselves without the need for the RAF.

Allied forces would be going backwards from now on for several months and it would be well into 1942 before they were able to stabilise some sort of defensive front. However, the Japanese still intended to force the issue and head towards India. British and Indian troops stood in their way, but it would be the RAF, by supporting and sustaining them, that would enable them to hold and fight back.

CHAPTER ONE
Caught on the Hop

While the thought that Japan might well start aggressive moves in 1941, or perhaps 1942, when they began on Sunday, 7 December 1941, with the surprise and unannounced attack on the US Naval Base at Pearl Harbor, Hawaii, it came as a complete shock. The only stroke of luck on that day, the day President F. D. Roosevelt called 'a day of infamy', was that the American aircraft carriers were at sea. Had they been in Pearl Harbor and been sunk or seriously damaged in the attack, it would have been a disaster, and the war in the Pacific would have turned out very differently in 1942.

The British, too, were completely surprised when, on 8 December, the Japanese made an initial troop landing at Kota Bharu, Malaya, then made an air raid upon Singapore and Hong Kong as well. On the 10th, Japanese aeroplanes attacked and sank two British capital ships, the *Prince of Wales* and *Repulse*, off the Malayan coast, an event that resounded loudly, not only locally but to their Lordships at the Admiralty in London.

In anticipation that something might happen, the RAF had despatched pilots and aircraft out to the Far East by a tortuous route in early September 1941. This route was from Liverpool by sea to Takoradi on the West African coast, thence flying across Africa in small numbers to Cairo with numerous stops to refuel. At Cairo the pilots lost their Hurricanes and boarded an Empire flying boat, flying to Basra, via Baghdad, then on to Karachi. A change of aeroplane took the pilots to Singapore Island, via Calcutta, Akyab, on the Bay of Bengal, Bangkok, Penang and finally Singapore, and the airfield at Kallang.

At Singapore already was No.488 Squadron RNZAF, formed early in September in New Zealand, the cadre being despatched to Singapore by sea. Its CO was Squadron Leader W. G. Clouston DFC, a Battle of Britain pilot. The arrival of pilots from Liverpool on the 29th saw Clouston's two flight commanders take up their positions: John Mackenzie DFC, another BofB veteran, and J. R. Hutcheson RNZAF. To their dismay they discovered they were to be equipped with Brewster Buffalo aircraft, for Mackenzie, a fighter far removed from the Spitfires he had flown in Britain. These three senior officers quickly put their pilots into a serious training regime. No sooner had the news arrived about Pearl Harbor, followed by a brief air raid the next day, the squadron was put on full alert and began to fly standing patrols.

Kallang also housed No. 243 Squadron and 453 Squadron RAAF was at nearby Sembawang. No. 453's temporary commander, Flight Lieutenant Tim Vigors, had won his DFC in the Battle of Britain, and Frank Howell, CO of 243, had also been awarded the DFC in that battle, and would end up as a prisoner of the Japanese. Along with the American Volunteer Group, these units would wage a brief but deadly war against the Japanese air forces before they had to fly their remaining aircraft away, shortly before the island surrendered. The most successful fighter pilot over Singapore was Sergeant G. B. Fisken RNZAF, flying with 243 Squadron. He would claim five enemy aircraft shot down with one probable and one damaged, plus another with 453 Squadron. Wounded on 1 February 1942, he was evacuated before the surrender.

The Buffalo squadrons on Singapore Island on Christmas Day 1941 were:

No.243 Sqn	15 aircraft commanded by S/Ldr F. J. Howell DFC (Kallang)
No.453 Sqn	18 aircraft commanded by Fl/Lt T. A. Vigors DFC (Sembawang)
No.488 Sqn	17 aircraft commanded by S/Ldr W. G. Clouston DFC (Kallang)

Another newly-formed Squadron, 136, had been on its way to the Middle East but with Japan's entry into the war, was diverted quickly and, by a similar route, the pilots found themselves in Cairo, from where, rather piecemeal, they headed for Singapore. Other squadrons too were on their way to the Middle East, 17 and 135, and they were also diverted, but with virtually no aircraft. Rather than Singapore, these were routed towards Rangoon. However, it was all taking a long time. The CO of 135 was Squadron Leader Frank Carey DFC DFM, an experienced fighter pilot, having seen action in both France and the Battle of Britain. He arrived at Rangoon (Mingaladon airfield) in the middle of an air raid on 19 January 1942. His pilots, meanwhile, were strung out somewhere behind him and not all would arrive before the retreat began. The first Hurricanes arrived on the 23rd.

Meantime, Singapore had fallen. The Japanese advanced from the north of the Malay peninsula and fought their way down. They suffered casualties from the guns of Singapore, including those facing south, many of which traversed to engage land targets, although their ammunition was designed for use against naval targets. The commander of Singapore did not surrender until the Japanese were in control of the island's water supply. Thousands of men marched into prison camps, including those who had arrived by sea just a short time before. It was a massive and humiliating defeat for the British in their Far East Empire.

Now having congregated at Rangoon, the RAF started to plan for the next line of defence. Pilots were still arriving from the UK piecemeal. Another Battle of Britain veteran to arrive was Squadron Leader T. A. F. Elsdon DFC, leader of 136. He and the CO of 17 Squadron, Squadron Leader C. A. C. Stone DFC, who'd seen action in the Battle of France, arrived at Rangoon, again with many of their pilots strewn out behind them, still on their eastward journeys. These two, plus Carey, and a few other early arrivals, were in action within days. Another unit at Mingaladon was 67 Squadron. They had been at Kallang until October, moving to Rangoon, taking their Buffalos with them. No. 67 also had a detachment on Ramu Island, commanded by Squadron Leader R. A. Milward DFC, who had won his decoration commanding 30 Squadron in Greece in the first months of 1941.

With the pending fall of Rangoon, the RAF and AVG pulled out on 2 March, heading north to Magwe and Akyab. As Rangoon fell on the 8th, the retreat through Burma had begun. These elements and the retreating British army were harried day after day by Japanese aircraft and advancing Japanese troops. In spite of the fear of capture there were organised defensive actions, especially at Yenangyaung and, with meagre supplies, little chance of a determined resistance could be contemplated seriously. Heavy air raids upon Magwe on the 21st and 22nd crippled Allied air power in Burma, and men who then retreated to Akyab were attacked on the 23rd. The next outpost, Toungoo, fell on the 30th, followed by Prome on 2 April.

The retreat continued, the Japanese taking Yenangyaung in mid-April, and then Mandalay on 1 May. The RAF evacuated across the border into India, Akyab was evacuated, Myitkyina (pronounced *Michinar*) fell on 8 May, Kalewa on the 10th. Finally the Japanese advance petered out and the front was stabilised somewhere between Rathedaung and Buthidaung. Inland from these places, and stretching east are range upon range of steep, long hills, with two major rivers dividing some of them, the

Irrawaddy to the south and the Chindwin farther north. This area is the Arakan, and the RAF would fly and operate over it for the next two years, and also down the Arakan coast, that edges onto the Bay of Bengal.

Meanwhile, reinforcements begin to arrive, both pilots and aeroplanes. Yet Burma was still at the far end of the food chain. There were virtually no permanent airfields here. The RAF would have to operate out of what were little more than fighter strips, often only drained rice paddy fields where the dividing bunds had been bulldozed flat, flat enough anyway for a landing field. Naturally there were no permanent buildings, certainly nothing even close to the nice brick and cement structures found in England. Pilots and ground crew lived in native 'bashas' – huts made out of bamboo and palm fronds. There were no aircraft hangars, so all maintenance was done out in the open, or at best, under some trees with perhaps a tarpaulin roped between them as cover. Food was poor and scarce. Spare parts and tools were at a premium. Changing an engine was a nightmare. Heatstroke, jungle sores, dysentery, dengi fever, malaria became part and parcel of the men's daily life in Burma. There were also tigers about, and elephants occasionally roamed through living areas, while in the monsoon periods everything became soaked and difficult to dry properly. As far as the fighting men in Burma were concerned, the Japanese, the main enemy, was way down the list of problems they faced.

The fighter defence of Singapore Island, at Kallang airfield, comprised Brewster Buffalo aircraft. This is a line-up of Buffalos of 453 Squadron RAAF, a unit that would be virtually wiped out over Malaya, Singapore and Batavia.

Brewster Buffalo of No. 67 Squadron, W.8245, marked, unusually with a dot after the W. The rectangular panel just ahead of the cockpit is of a Kiwi, denoting the pilot was probably a New Zealander. The machine survived until finally Struck off Charge (SOC) in November 1943.

Another 67 Squadron Buffalo, this one (W8243) in flight over Kallang airfield in December 1941.

A Squadron of P-40 Tomahawks of the AVG was also based at Singapore. Known as the *Flying Tigers*, they carried shark mouths on and around the large air intake, and a shark's eye above. The American volunteers who flew them received cash payments from the Chinese for each Japanese aeroplane they shot down. Not unnaturally, some of their claims were a trifle exaggerated.

Flight Lieutenant John Mackenzie DFC in front of his Buffalo. This New Zealander had fought in the Battle of Britain and became one of those fighting airmen who saw action through virtually the whole war. After a period in New Zealand, he returned to the UK to fly Spitfires again, including D-Day operations, and in 1945, back in NZ, was converting to Corsairs for operations in the Pacific when the war ended.

Pilots of 488 RNZAF Squadron at Singapore in 1941. (L to R) Mackenzie, John Hutcheson, Terry Honan, Jack Meharry, Jack Godstiff (kneeling), Frank Johnstone, E. W. Cox, Eddie Kuhn, Vern Meaclem (head only), Tiny White, Burt Pettit, Wally Greenhalgh, Perce Killick, Jack Burton, Don Clow, Pete Gifford (kneeling), Derek Charters, and Len Farr.

Japanese attacks on Kallang airfield quickly reduced the fighting strength there. This severely damaged Buffalo has been raised on to supports but it was a hopeless task for the maintenance crews.

Hurricane fighters began to arrive in January 1942, but it was too little too late. This Hurricane was quickly damaged and is under repair. Out in the open, aircraft were always vulnerable to attacks from Japanese aircraft.

Burning Buffalo aircraft on Kallang airfield. Any thought of a stiff defence of the island base of Singapore was quickly quashed.

Pilots of 17 Squadron outside their dispersal hut at Kallang. Note the variety of dress, from shirts, slacks, overalls and, of course, the obligatory pith helmet. The wearing of side-arms had also become the norm.

Just before Singapore fell, any surviving aeroplanes were flown north to Rangoon or out to places such as Penang and Sumatra. The RAF intended to make a stand from Mingaladon airfield, Rangoon. It was now that the long-awaited reinforcements began to trickle in from the UK. Among the first to arrive was Squadron Leader C. A. C. Stone DFC. 'Bunny' Stone, seen here seated in his Hurricane with squadron leader's pennant painted by the cockpit, shot down a Japanese bomber on 24 January, and damaged two more. Two days later he downed another during a night raid.

Other early arrivals were Ken Hemingway, M. C. 'Bush' Cotton and Frank Carey DFC DFM. Hemingway later wrote the book *Wings over Burma*, and 'Bush' Cotton came from Australia. Note the tennis rackets!

In order to fly in Hurricanes from far afield, Cairo via India, they were fitted with long-range fuel tanks. These tanks were non-jettisonable and had to be physically removed on the ground. Some of the first to arrive were sent up to engage Japanese raiders almost immediately, the pilots seriously handicapped by these appendages.

Another Hurricane with underwing tanks. To ensure they wouldn't be surprised on the ground, the aircraft is being refuelled so that it can get off if an air raid developed.

A reinforcement Hurricane arrives (Z4726). It is identified by a crudely applied number 2 on the fuselage, possibly with whitewash. It was damaged in action over Rangoon on 23 January 1942, being flown by Bunny Stone, having been one of the first three Hurricanes to reach Burma.

Ken Bunting, from Yorkshire, in his 136 Squadron Hurricane. He ferried at least one of the reinforcement aircraft into Rangoon.

Other early arrivals of 136 Squadron pilots were (L to R) Gordon Conway, L. H. 'Dopey' LeCraw, Freddie Fortune and C. J. 'Winky' Moorhouse.

Squadron Leader Frank Carey, in regulation pith helmet, at Rangoon. Seated in the jeep with him is Major R. H. 'Bob' Neale of the AVG. Note the AVG Tomahawk in the background. Despite the serious situation in which they found themselves, they could still smile for the camera. Frank Carey destroyed a Japanese fighter over Mingaladon on 29 January, and destroyed six more Japanese aircraft during February, bringing his personal score to twenty-eight.

Burning aircraft on Mingaladon airfield. It was Singapore all over again.

A 135 Squadron Hurricane IIB on Mingaladon airfield, February 1942. The squadron still carried its European identity code letters WK. Later in this year the marking of aircraft with squadron identification letters was stopped and only an individual aircraft letter was carried. This was in order to fool the Japanese. It was hoped that being unable to identify squadrons they might believe there were more squadrons in theatre than there actually were. Sometime in 1944 the unit letters returned as by then there were many more squadrons in Burma.

Another early arrival was Squadron Leader T. A. F. 'Taffy' Elsdon DFC, CO of 136 Squadron, known as the 'Woodpeckers'. Elsdon, on the right, was a Battle of Britain veteran, and known as Chief Woodpecker. On the left is Squadron Leader A. W. Ridler, who took over 136 in July 1942.

CHAPTER TWO

Retreat from Rangoon

Now that the RAF was retreating into India, through a region known as the Arakan, British and Indian troops began finally to stem the advance of Japanese troops invading farther north from Burma. For several days the RAF had been scattered across various parts of Burma, retreating via bases at Prome, Magwe, Akyab and Toungoo.

The main concentration of RAF aircraft would eventually be established at Chittagong on the Arakan coast, and also at Cox's Bazar, also on the coast but farther south. Pilots and ground crews had many adventures during this retreat, mostly travelling by road, some by ship and others by air. A few flew out in a Bristol Bombay, while some even went off in an ancient Vickers Valentia. Some had lucky escapes, others didn't. Nos 17 and 135 Squadrons had set up BurWing, or MagWing, at Magwe, with just sixteen Hurricane IIs (plus some AVG P-40s), while 136 and some of 135 Squadron had set up AkWing at Akyab. No.136 Squadron, had just nine Hurricane Is, and one Hurricane II; it had ten of its original pilots and five new arrivals who had been gravitating towards Burma for some time. The Hurricane Is had been issued from an Operational Training Unit, all reputedly deemed 'fit for training only'! It was suspected that some Hurricanes were being retained at Calcutta for local defence, so Frank Carey was sent to find out. He did, and they were, and even distant Karachi was found to be keeping some too.

Warning systems were very rudimentary and there was almost no way of being prepared for Japanese aircraft attacking the airstrips. Small units were set up in the hills to the east, reporting any sign of enemy action, but there was no radar, and any warning was simply by radio. Any change of direction by passing raiders would often go un-noticed and, therefore, un-reported.

RAF fighters and light bombers made occasional forays into Burma to attack Japanese bases, but these were very hit and miss. The Japanese usually pulled their aircraft back so as not to be at risk from British air attack, only returning when they intended to make a raid. The AVG also made strafing attacks on occasion, and on 19 March 1942 they attacked Moulmein aerodrome, claiming a number of enemy aircraft destroyed on the ground.

RAF fighters were still in short supply, and it became clear that authorities in Calcutta, and even as far as Karachi on the western side of India, were continuing to keep some back for local defence rather than let them continue to northern Burma. Hurricanes were also being used for reconnaissance as far south as Rangoon even though it was obvious that the Allies were going to have to remain in the Arakan for some time before there was any hope of an advance back towards southern Burma. Pilots were still arriving in theatre, but tools and spares were continuing to be in short supply, and unserviceable Hurricanes quickly became 'Christmas Trees' as their working bits and pieces were cannibalised to keep others flying.

Once the RAF established itself along a defence line in the Arakan, nature came to the aid of Allied forces with the arrival of the annual monsoon. During March each year a gentle wind rises south of the Equator, heads north and meets the heat of Asia. By May this wind arrives over the Bay of Bengal and clouds of moisture rise from the sea. With the Himalayas blocking its path farther north, the moisture unloads over Burma. Normal life becomes severely affected and for the RAF life was to become even more difficult. With no permanent aircraft hangars, all servicing had to be done out in the open, and the airstrips quickly became quagmires of mud. Everything was damp and remained so. However, it halted the Japanese advance too, which would have to wait until later in the year for clearer weather. Several squadrons moved farther north, to the Calcutta area, based at Jessore (17), Dum Dum (135) and Alipore (136). Others went to Baigachi. Frank Carey became a wing commander, 135 being taken over by Squadron Leader F. B. Sutton DFC. Carey would later become the boss of a fighter training establishment at Amarda Road, Orissa, after leading Fighter Wings at Alipore, Dum Dum and Chittagong.

Gradually during this lull in operations, more and more Hurricanes began to trickle through, and so too did further squadrons. These new arrivals still had the tortuous routes to follow, either via Freetown on the west coast of Africa, or via Durban, on the South African coast before sailing to Karachi. Nos. 607 and 615 Squadrons were two of the new arrivals, commanded by Squadron Leader N. J. Mowat DSO and Squadron Leader B. L. Duckenfield AFC. Both had seen action during the Battle of

Britain, and Mowat, a New Zealander, had won his DSO during operations against the German capital ships' 'Channel Dash' in February 1942. No.607 went to Alipore, 615 to Jessore. No.79 Squadron, arrived and went to Kanchrapara, north of Calcutta, commanded by Squadron Leader C. A. T. Jones who had seen action over Dunkirk and been wounded during the Battle of Britain.

Everyone now had time to settle down, prepare for future operations once the monsoon cleared, and have time to fully realise that Burma was a lot different from Britain. If it wasn't clear at this stage, it would soon become evident that pilots and ground personnel in Burma could look forward to being stuck here for a long time.

* *

In mid-1942, one of the fighter squadrons was given a very different job to handle, the defence of Calcutta. Despite there being a number of airfields about the city, the population was extremely nervous in case Japanese bombers started raiding. What was needed was not only the close presence of a squadron, but one that the populace could actually see. In the centre of Calcutta ran a wide thoroughfare called Red Road, in the Maidan district – bang in the centre. It ran parallel to the city's main street of Chowringhee. Provided it was closed to civilian traffic, it was long and wide enough to permit Hurricanes to land there. Along one side too was an open area where aircraft could be dispersed, plus a tree-lined area. No.136 Squadron got the job. Although everyone called it Red Road, it was officially named the 'Maidan Strip' and Wing Commander Carey made the first attempt at getting a Hurricane safely down upon it, making his approach down Old Courthouse Street. He did so without too much difficulty and soon afterwards, the rest of 136 flew in. The pilots were billeted in the Grand Hotel and, if nothing else, it was a lot better than the Arakan fighter strips. Over time, other squadrons took turns to be based there, but the Woodpeckers were the first.

A 67 Squadron Hurricane that did not survive Magwe. A Dakota in the background awaits evacuation. The Hurricane has overshot some form of pipeline that ended its landing run.

The airstrip at Akyab, looking east-south-east. Notice the absence of any form of permanent buildings.

Hawker Hurricane coming in to land at a strip named 'Auld Angus' near Akyab, March 1942. The pilot is Squadron Leader Jimmy Elsdon DFC, CO of 136 Squadron.

Pilot Officer H. J. 'Snooks' Everard of 17 Squadron, got into a fight with enemy fighters over Magwe on 21 March and claimed one destroyed and another damaged. Unfortunately, he then fired at a PRU Hurricane flown by K. A. Perkin, that he assumed was another Japanese fighter. Perkin force-landed by a river at Yenangyaung, near Magwe, luckily without injury. Perkin, of No.2 PRU, went on to command a Hurricane squadron.

'Snooks' Everard RCAF (right) with Pilot Officer L. H. 'Dopey' LeCraw RCAF of 136 Squadron. Everard went on to fly over Italy, and win the DFC, then flew in Northern Europe in 1944 until brought down and captured. LeCraw was wounded and baled out on 27 March 1942. Landing in the sea he found it impossible to inflate his Mae West as he had holes in both cheeks and could not blow.

Sergeant V. B. G. Butler was badly shot about in an air battle near Akyab on 23 March 1942 but made a successful crash-landing despite having much of the fabric burnt off the top of his Hurricane's fuselage.

Vern Butler, 136 Squadron, often referred to as 'Rhet' from his similar looks to film star Clark Gable. Vern was killed at Imphal in 1944, shot down by a Japanese Oscar.

Pilots of 67 Squadron. (l to r) Sergeant C. W. 'Speed' Elliott, Flight Lieutenant Ken Hemingway, Flying Officer Pete Hanan, Squadron Leader J. M. Bachmann (killed in action 9 April 1943), Sergeant B. N. Buckley (wounded 31 May 1943), Don Mercer and Rex Rudkin.

Pilots of 136 Squadron on 27 May 1942. (rear l to r) Frank Wilding, T. T. Young (killed in flying accident with 79 Squadron, November 1942), Kit Kitley, Guy Marsland, Squadron Leader Elsdon, Winky Moorhouse, Benny Banikhin (killed in a flying accident [KIFA] in October 1942), 'Ting' Bunting; front: Hamish Wetheral, Chas Beale, 'Biff' Veins, Vern Butler (KIA March 1944). Just a few hours later, Wetheral was killed after his Hurricane developed a glycol leak and crashed.

Australian Flight Lieutenants M. C. C. Cotton RAAF and F. B. Sutton. Barry Sutton became CO of 135 Squadron in February 1942. He had seen action in the Battle of Britain and is the author of the book *The Way of a Pilot.* Later flew as a wing leader at Imphal and received the DFC in 1945. 'Bush' Cotton flew Hurricanes in the UK before being posted to 17 Squadron. Wounded in action on 27 February 1942, he had shot down a bomber before being shot about by ten enemy fighters. He received the DFC.

Squadron Leader Basil Duckenfield AFC, CO of 615 Squadron, talking to Group Captain Seton Broughall MC DFC (who had been OC Mingaladon), and Wing Commander H. M. Stephen DSO DFC, Battle of Britain pilot, Wing Commander Flying at Dum Dum, and later Jessore.

Squadron Leader Noel Mowat DSO, CO of 607 Squadron, 1941-43.

Pilots of 79 Squadron (l to r): Gatty May, Duffy, Flight Lieutenant R. E. Mason, Squadron Leader C. A. T. Jones, Sir Thomas Lamb, Flight Lieutenant Guy Hogan, Flying Officer R. H. H. 'Russ' Bowes, Flying Officer 'Windy' Mears, and Pilot Officer O. J. Hodgson.

Flight Lieutenant G. J. C. Hogan's Hurricane IIB with four 20mm cannon and tropical air filter, on Chittagong airfield.

Guy Hogan. In 1944 he would be awarded the DFC for his leadership of No. 5 Squadron in attacking ground targets and Japanese transport.

Pilots of 135 Squadron (rear l to r): Flying Officer Malcolm McRae (killed in flying accident January 1943), Bill Brown, Bill Bedford, James Madle, Hughie Dean; front: Lee Hawkins and Ray Prince. Bill Bedford later became a test pilot, working on 'the flying bedstead' that eventually led to the development of the Hawker Harrier jump-jet.

Pilots of 607 Squadron (l to r): Sergeant K. F. Longley, Warrant Officer R. W. Bobby Bates, Sergeant W. A. Goold, Squadron Leader R. H. Holland DFC, (CO), Pilot Officer K. Clark, Pilot Officer W. B. Gibbs and Flying Officer C. T. Doudy. Bobby Holland had won his DFC in the Battle of Britain and Wi[illegible] Goold and Colin Doudy, both Australians, would receive DFC[illegible] for their actions over Burma

Hurricanes of 136 Squadron parked beneath trees near the Red Road, Calcutta. Note the Woodpecker insignia on the engine cowling, and an Indian soldier standing guard. June 1942.

Another view of Woodpecker Hurricanes at Red Road, August 1942. There is a makeshift sentry box in front of the tree and another guard in front of the right-hand fighter.

CHAPTER THREE

Life on the Airstrips

As previously mentioned, Allied airmen arriving from their home countries where they had become used to permanent, solid, brick-built buildings for accommodation, offices, aircraft hangars, administrative sections, messes, and so on, had quickly to come to terms with a very different situation in Burma. Heat was another factor, especially for the British airman, used to indifferent weather with a good deal of cold and penetrating damp atmosphere. For the ground crews who had to keep the aeroplanes in the air, they could no longer indent for whatever piece of equipment or spare part they needed. There was going to be a delay whatever happened. Certain stocks would be kept back in mainland India, but even there they were dependent on the long supply route from Britain.

It almost goes without saying that the British airmen adapted quickly to their new situation and surroundings, and with their normal aplomb, got on with it, determined to make the best of a bad situation. However, where in Britain they might occasionally go down with a cold, or even a bout of influenza from time to time, the list of things they could get in this part of the Far East was many and varied, and almost everything was extremely debilitating. Working on the airstrips, mechanics in the heat of summer, would almost universally be attired in little else but shorts, suede jungle boots and a pith helmet or sloppy hat. Pilots would also wear shorts, shirt and shoes or boots, but when on operations or on stand-by, generally wore khaki slacks, sturdy shoes or flying boots, mindful of the lower temperatures they would encounter once airborne.

Rather than batmen, or even batwomen, in RAF messes in the UK, most of the support personnel were local natives, Indian or Burmese, who would cook, clean, wash and iron for a few rupees. They would strip the charpoys [beds] daily, air and dry the bed-sheets, make sure any creepy-crawlies were brushed out and generally maintain some degree of comfort for their officers and men. In this chapter we shall briefly examine some of the extremes of difference from Britain and Burma.

As mentioned earlier, the Japanese were certainly down the list of problems for the RAF men in Burma. Irregular supplies of food, spare parts, engines, suitable accommodation, and protection from the heat and monsoon rains, all made life far from bearable. It is a miracle they endured for so long, for there were no long periods of leave and one could not expect an early return to family and loved ones. That would only come with victory in the Far East. Or serious injury or illness.

Food was often supplemented by hunting parties armed with Lee Enfield .303 rifles. Men would trek into the jungle and try to shoot birds, even game if some could be found. The sighting of the occasional tiger paw-print helped concentrate the mind during these forays. There was little room for the niceties. One visiting senior officer went along on one of these expeditions, and was appalled that the men actually shot birds sitting on branches rather than on the wing! Disease was rife, especially malaria. Insects and ants plagued everything. Legs of charpoys had to be set in small tins filled with petrol in order to prevent bugs crawling up them. Mosquito netting had to be secured while sleeping, leaving no gaps for anything to fly in and bite. Hot baths became a distant memory, shaving often tortuous. It says volumes for the pilots and airmen that they cheerfully kept going, determined to defeat the Japanese and prevent them marching into India.

In the hot months it was dust that had to be contended with; in the monsoon it was mud. Jungle boots gave way to rubber boots in the wet. Later in the war, when Americans began arriving, RAF personnel were amazed at just what they brought with them. Refrigerators, ice-making machines, Coca-Cola, and all manner of goodies to eat, such as marmalade, that the RAF boys had long since forgotten even existed.

There is another story of a senior officer arriving on a visit from Delhi to a front-line airstrip. Walking with the CO of the resident squadron, an airman strolled by carrying some piece of equipment on one shoulder. The airman nodded, smiled, and winked at the two men. The Delhi man was aghast, and made comment. The CO agreed, saying, 'I know, the buggers don't even salute me!'

An RAF airman once recalled to me that after several days lying on his charpoy with severe dysentery, he finally felt sufficiently well to go for a stroll. All went well until he returned to his tent, around which he had fashioned a small ridge of earth to prevent rain water running into it. Feeling very happy, he gaily skipped over the 'bung' whereupon his bowels emptied as he hit the ground.

This picture could have been taken anywhere on a Burmese or Arakan airstrip. A combination of native 'basha' huts, tents or plain tarpaulin coverings, anything that would keep out any precipitation that might occur. These would be erected inside the tree line away from the runway areas, the guy ropes being ideal for hanging out washing or airing sheets

A typical airman's bed in a tent or similar sleeping area. The airman, Jack Kemp of 615 Squadron, has tried to make himself as comfortable as possible, using a trunk in which to store his clothing and other personal items. This looks a little staged, possibly due for an inspection, but one can see matting on the ground, a pair of shoes, gumboots, horse-hair pillows and a blanket or two. Family pictures remind him of home and loved ones, who he will not see for months, if not years.

Stormy weather, especially high winds, would cause much damage to these very flimsy structures, and sudden downpours, certainly during a monsoon, would soak everything within seconds. Monsoon rain has been described as akin to someone emptying a swimming pool on you!

Even on the more established airfields, such as this scene at Chittagong, the men were still faced with further variations of native basha huts and accommodation. These were aircrew quarters for 136 Squadron.

Bashas amongst the trees. At least they provided some slight protection in case of a Japanese surprise air attack. They all came with associated jungle noises from birds, animals and insects.

The airman who took this picture included his bearer, a young Burmese lad, looking quizzically at the camera. Again guy ropes provide something on which to hang washing, and the obligatory china teapot gives at least a feel of far off England. Note, too, the rudimentary attempt at some camouflage paint on the tent's roof. In the lower foreground is a charpoy (bed).

Inside a larger tent used as a mess. This time we have a metal teapot, and even milk jugs. Plates, cups and saucers, napkins, and familiar looking jam and sauce pots give an appearance of home. Tablecloths also give a feel of normality and standards. Note the waiter in the background, and another by the entrance, serving tea to the officers. Third from the left, far side, is Squadron Leader C. M. Crothers, Senior Admin Officer of 165 Fighter Wing. On the nearside, from left, is Major Phillips, an army liaison officer, second from left is Flying Officer Pattinson, Wing Armament Officer.

In the Arakan there was no place to sneak off and have a bath, as would have been the norm in the UK. The best that could be hoped for, unless a spot of leave in Calcutta came along, was a hip bath out in the open. With boyish enthusiasm, friends would delight in sneaking up to take a photograph of the unfortunate bather. Here, Squadron Leader C. A. T. Jones, CO of 79 Squadron, is caught adding water to his nether regions. One can imagine what he is saying, probably ending in 'off!'

Flight Lieutenant Art Brown RCAF of 258 Squadron, is also caught out. He was killed during a Japanese raid on Calcutta on 5 December 1943, not by enemy action but, it was assumed, oxygen failure, resulting in him diving steeply into the Indian Ocean.

Flying Officer D. A. 'Benny' Benson, 607 Squadron, caught out in the open at Wangjing, in the Imphal Valley. Note, too, the other piece of kit, a washstand.

Flight Sergeant Bill Hinton, 135 Squadron, at Dohazari. At least he has managed to acquire a tin bath, similar to those often found in the UK, and used in front of a roaring fire. Note the flying boots and, just as in the UK, a bicycle to get around on. Hinton shot down an Oscar on 10 December 1942.

Flight Lieutenant Graham Falconer RAAF, 615 Squadron, seems less than amused, but at least he has a tin bath. His bearer is named as Munsing. Note that the bath is situated near a water pump – luxury!

Wilf Goold RAAF, of 607 Squadron, can do little more than smile at the camera. Note his leather washing-kit holder and possibly a razor kit too.

Two 136 Squadron airmen sit on the rear of a Hurricane while the pilot guns the engine to check for any sign of a magneto drop. At least this is one case where a pith helmet is useful. This Hurricane, BH142, was damaged in air combat on 10 December 1942; flown by Bill Davis it was lost to enemy action in April 1943.

It appears to take four men to oil a 136 Squadron tail fin, one to do the job, three to oversee it's done properly. Note a line of native workers in the background.

Outdoor engine maintenance in the correct dress, shorts and pith helmet. The lack of a ladder is overcome by the use of an oil drum.

An armourer working on a Hurricane's 20mm cannon. The brickwork underfoot suggests the picture was taken while 136 Squadron was on the Red Road, Calcutta.

There was always time to sleep and, as it was sometimes difficult to sleep in the sticky heat of the night, pilots catnapped when they could. Here Squadron Leader Jimmy Elsdon prefers a nod to his newspaper.

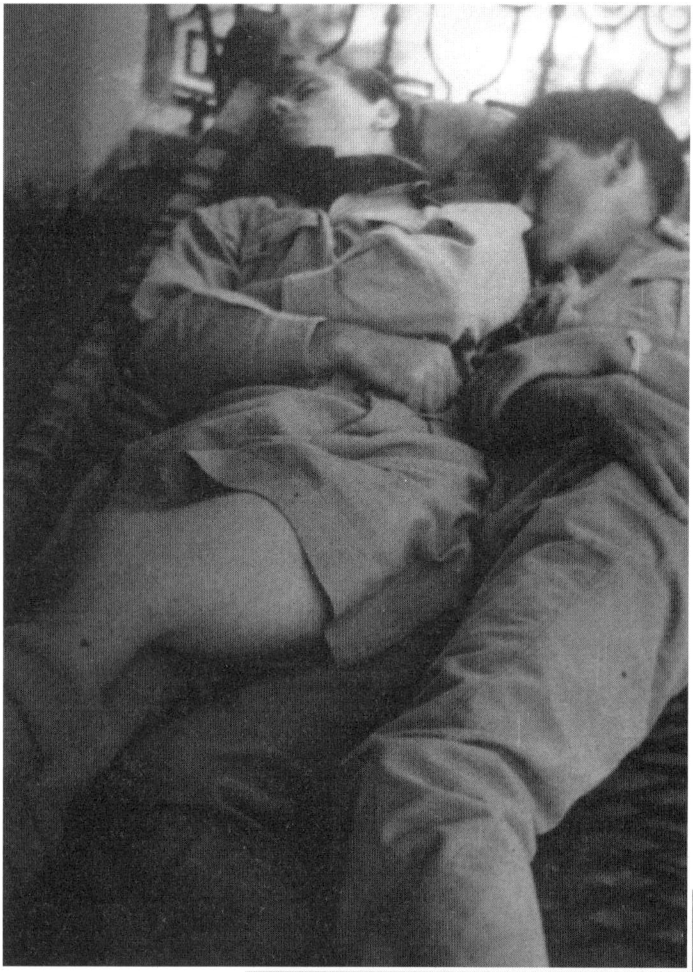

Ray Prince and Eric Batchelor, 135 Squadron, share a daytime siesta on a charpoy. Tragically, Prince was killed on 11 March 1943. On an air test he crept up on another Hurricane, the pilot of which thought he was being attacked by a Japanese fighter, turned and shot Prince down.

Flying Officer A. J. H. Kitley, 136 Squadron, catches some 'zeds'. The original caption suggests he was 'At Readiness'. Alan Kitley later served with 9 Squadron, Indian Air Force.

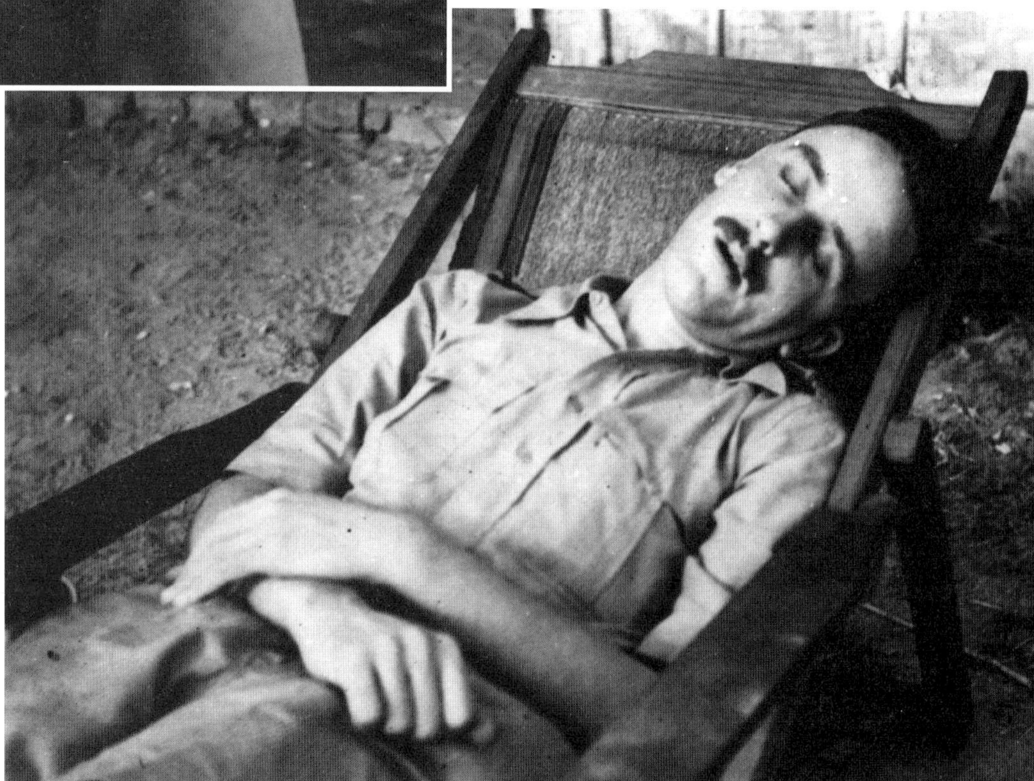

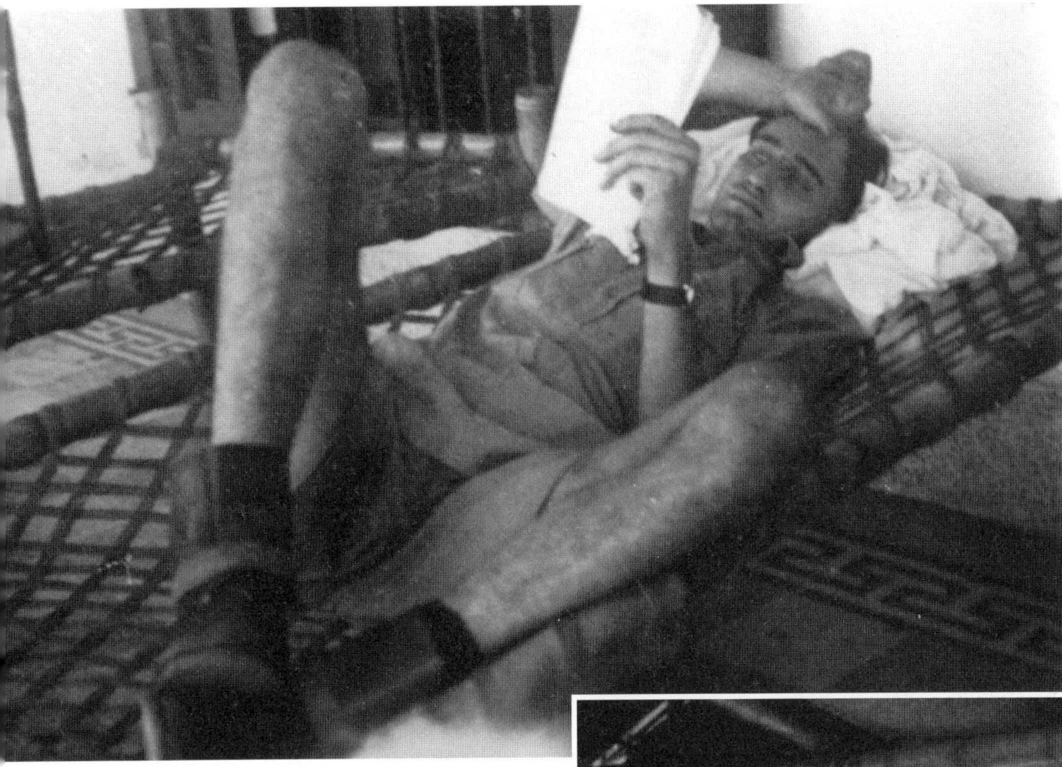

Letters from home were always welcome. Warrant Officer A. J. 'Bing' De Cruyenaere, RCAF but of Belgian extraction, was killed in action with 136 Squadron on 15 March 1943, shot down by a Japanese fighter.

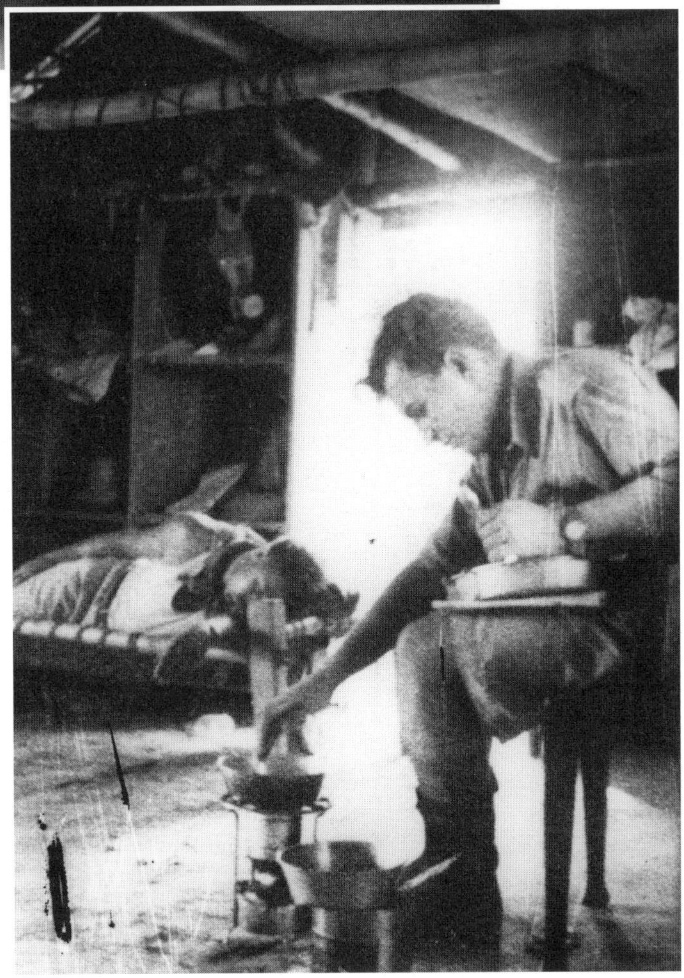

If you want something to eat, get it yourself. 'Ting' Bunting heats up a meal on a primus stove in his quarters. Eric Brown snoozes on his charpoy.

Airmen of 135 Squadron erecting their sleeping quarters on an airstrip in the Arakan.

Leading Aircraftman Les Jones, armourer with 135 Squadron, posing in the cockpit of a Hurricane. The side panel is off to access the transmitter/receiver.

A 135 Squadron Hurricane (Z5659) with its ground crew: Leading Aircraftman L. J. Jones, armourer, is on the left. This fighter was struck off charge on 7 July 1943.

CHAPTER FOUR

The First Arakan Campaign

The area known as the Arakan, above which much bitter fighting would be seen over the next two years, bordered the Bay of Bengal on its western side. It ran from the Chin Hills on the edge of Manipur, down to the south-west corner of Burma. The main area of activity was a relatively narrow strip, stretching south from the Indian border to the island and town of Akyab, which the Japanese had taken over as their main base. Cox's Bazar lay ten miles to the north of Akyab, with Chittagong forty-five miles farther on. The jungle-clad Mayu mountain range, that dominates the Mayu peninsula, situated roughly between the ports of Chittagong and Akyab, rises some 2,000 feet, and is about eighty miles in length. Farther inland to the east is a series of hills and valleys running north to south and any journey on foot in either direction, east or west, meant climbing and descending them. Any pilot who came down inland, and was forced to walk back, had these to contend with, in addition to thick jungle, streams and rivers.

Things were relatively quiet over the Arakan during September to November 1942, as the monsoon at first raged and then lessened. Occasionally, as weather permitted, Blenheim light bombers might raid Japanese bases and, during this phase, while Hurricanes were still arriving piecemeal into India, Curtiss Mohawk fighters of 5 and 155 Squadrons, escorted the bombers. Their only drawback was that, having radial engines, they could be mistaken for Japanese Mitsubishi 0 (Zero) fighters or Nakajima 01 (Ki-43) fighters, Allied code name Oscar. Zero fighters were Navy aircraft, Oscars Army. It was these Army fighters that were encountered over Burma, but were occasionally referred to, wrongly, as Zeros.

The Hurricanes of 607 Squadron had become operational in July 1942 and by September were sending detachments to the airfield at Feni (in truth little more than a dirt strip) where they could protect against any Japanese approaches to Calcutta from the east. No.615 Squadron too became operational and also provided sections to operate from Feni, which was situated well north of Chittagong, just west of today's border between India and Bangladesh, and about twenty miles from the coast.

As the weather improved both British and Japanese army commanders were planning offensives on the Arakan. The Japanese needed to continue their push north, into India, while the British and Indian forces needed to counter-attack south towards Akyab. It would soon be a case of who struck first. In preparation, the RAF fighters not only moved into Feni but also to Agartala, just north of Feni. Although there were several fighter strips in the Arakan, others, such as 'George' and 'Hove' were opened up right on the beach south of Cox's Bazar. The sand was found to be solid enough to land fighters at these places.

During the lull, time and thought had been given to how to combat the Japanese aircraft, especially their fighters. The Zero was only met on a few occasions, being a Navy machine; the main opponent was the Army 01 (Ki-43) Oscar. In the first encounters with these nimble fighters over Singapore and Rangoon, experienced RAF pilots had tried to use tactics they had employed over France, Dunkirk and in the Battle of Britain, where Spitfires and Hurricanes could turn inside the German Messerschmitt 109s. However, the Japanese fighters were exceptionally light and could turn inside the Hurricanes. The Oscar did not carry radio, armour or self-sealing fuel tanks, which made them highly manoeuvrable. However, if they were hit, the damage sustained usually proved fatal. The trick of course was to hit them. The fighter pilots who had gained experience against Japanese fighters – and survived – now formulated tactics to combat them. Rather than a turning battle, the doctrine was to use 'dive and zoom' tactics. That is, dive, close, fire, and use the speed to pull up again, and hope to be able to repeat the manoeuvre if the opponent had not been shot down. In any event, it was usual for the Japanese to keep their aircraft well back from the front, and only bring them to forward airfields when about to launch a raid.

In September 1942, RAF fighter squadrons in India were as follows:

No.224 Group, Calcutta

No.5 Sqn	Dinjan	Mohawk	S/Ldr W. Pitt-Brown
No.17 Sqn	Alipore	Hurricane	S/Ldr J. H. Iremonger
No.67 Sqn	Alipore	Hurricane	S/Ldr J. H. Bachmann
No.136 Sqn	Alipore	Hurricane	S/Ldr A. W. Ridler
No.607 Sqn	Alipore	Hurricane	S/Ldr N. J. Mowat DSO
No.135 Sqn	Dum Dum	Hurricane	S/Ldr H. S. Giddings

No.146 Sqn	Jessore	Hurricane	S/Ldr M. B. Czernin DFC
No.615 Sqn	Jessore	Hurricane	S/Ldr B. L. Duckenfield AFC
No.79 Sqn	Kanchapara	Hurricane	S/Ldr C. A. Jones

There were also four Hurricane squadrons on the island of Ceylon (present day Sri Lanka), 30, 258, at Ratmalana, commanded by Squadron Leader A. W. A. Bayne DFC and Squadron Leader R. J. Walker, and 261 and 273 Squadrons at China Bay, commanded by Squadron Leader E. G. R. Downey and Squadron Leader A. N. Constantine.

* *

Both sides had begun bombing each other, and Japanese aircraft had raided Chittagong in early December. On 10 December 135 and 136 Squadrons had been in combat with enemy aircraft over Chittagong, Flight Sergeant F. W. T. 'Bill' Davis of 136 having his machine damaged, while 135 lost two pilots killed (Flying Officer J. Monk and Sergeant J. Goldney) and another Hurricane damaged. On the 15th, 79 Squadron had engaged Japanese bombers and fighters going for Chittagong, claiming three bombers and two fighters with others damaged. Squadron Leader C. A. Jones, Russ Bowes and Sergeant K. B. May got the bombers, Pilot Officer R. Gray and Sergeant R. L. North the Oscars. May also probably destroyed another bomber. In reality the claims were over-optimistic, but the Japanese pilots too exaggerated their claims, with six Hurricanes reported shot down whereas the RAF didn't suffer any losses.

Having gained the RAF's attention here, the Japanese then mounted an attack on Feni on the 16th. Little damage was done at Feni but RAF fighters met the raiding force and suffered casualties. Flight Lieutenant R. Hedderwick claimed one Oscar, while other pilots claimed four Sallys damaged (a Sally was a Mitsubishi Ki-21 Army Type 97 heavy bomber). However, two of 607's aircraft were shot down, with Robin Hedderwick, and Pilot Officer W. D. James injured. Two more Hurricanes had been damaged.

Meantime, the Japanese had begun their advance north, just beating the British plan to head south. The Japanese reached Buthidaung and then Maungdaw, villages that more or less constituted the front line in the Arakan. Japanese aircraft bombed Calcutta at night, something that so panicked the populace that thousands evacuated the town, seriously disrupting the Allied supply line. As these activities were in progress the British finally decided to make an advance, with Buthidaung and Maungdaw being their first objectives. The Japanese did indeed pull back, a move that encouraged a further advance south.

Blenheim bombers were flying bombing raids down to Akyab and Magwe, escorted by Hurricanes, and shortly after Christmas 1942, 615 and 136 Squadrons lost their COs while operating against these Japanese bases. Squadron Leader Bryon Duckenfield simply failed to return from an attack on Magwe on 28 December. He ended up as a prisoner of war, and after suffering a period of solitary confinement, was imprisoned in Rangoon. Former Battle of Britain pilot W. D. Williams DFC assumed command of 615 in January 1943. He had commanded one of the American Eagle squadrons briefly in 1942.

Squadron Leader Ridler went missing the very next day. He and Pilot Officer Ian Adamson headed down to Akyab, hoping to catch enemy aircraft on the airstrip, taking off before dawn with an airman swinging a lantern at the end of the airfield at Cox's Bazar, where the two Hurricane pilots had landed to refuel. By first light they had flown by Akyab, then turned so as to approach it from the south. However, they were flying so low that Ridley simply went into the sea and despite Adamson trying to find a sign of him he failed to do so. Adamson carried on, having a scare as his long range tanks ran dry, but quickly switched to mains. In the event, as he reached Akyab he found it covered in fog. Fortunately Ridler turned up a few days later, having bobbed to the surface with his Mae West inflated but he had smashed his face on the gun-sight, achieving what so many Hurricane pilots suffered, a broken nose. He had seen Adamson fly off but shortly afterwards some native fisherman came along and pulled him out of the water and set him on his way back north and to safety.

Initially the Allied advance went well and soon Akyab was in their sights. Unhappily, as the advance moved forward, the supply line became stretched, causing delays. Then unseasonal rain disrupted road traffic and so 1942 ended with the advance stalled at the end of the Mayu river, Akyab still tantalisingly out of reach.

In January 1943 the RAF had several fighter squadrons on the Arakan and these can be listed as follows:

No.165 Wing, Chittagong			
No.17 Sqn	Chittagong	Hurricane (6)	S/Ldr M. C. C. Cotton DFC
(rest of Squadron at Red Road, Calcutta)			
No.79 Sqn	Dohazari	Hurricane	S/Ldr C. A. Jones
No.135 Sqn	Nidania +	Hurricane	S/Ldr H. S. Giddings
No.136 Sqn	Chittagong	Hurricane	S/Ldr A. W. A. Bayne DFC
No.146 Sqn	Cox's Bazar	Hurricane	S/Ldr G. R. T. Williams
No.28 Sqn	Ranchi	Hurricane*	S/Ldr A. S. Mann
No.166 Wing, Feni			
No.607 Sqn	Feni	Hurricane	S/Ldr R. H. Holland DFC
No.615 Sqn	Feni	Hurricane	S/Ldr W. D. Williams DFC
No.167 Wing, Agartala			
No.5 Sqn	Agartala	Mohawk	S/Ldr P. M. Bond
No.155 Sqn	Agartala	Mohawk	S/Ldr C. G. St D. Jeffries DFC

+ Nidania was usually referred to as 'George' airstrip, right on the beach.
* No. 28 Squadron was flying reconnaissance and Tac/R missions. As well as Ranchi, north-west of Calcutta, it was operating detachments at both Imphal and Ramu.

RAF aircraft began supporting British and Indian ground forces in January, hoping to help a move forward, but the delay gave the Japanese time to build strong defensive positions in the Donbaik area on the coast of the Mayu peninsula and across the river at Rathedaung. In the air RAF and Japanese pilots fought in open combat over the jungles until the latter became scarce in the last week of February, but they were back in March, as their soldiers began a counter-offensive against the Allied troops on the 5th. It was a classic, and well proven, Japanese manoeuvre: infiltrate, encircle and force the enemy to retire.

The Japanese began from the eastern bank of the Mayu river and across the hills, succeeding in taking up positions behind forward British and Indian troops holding the Rathedaung front. Over the following days Japanese airmen achieved a measure of success in depriving Allied ground forces of the air cover they would have liked, as well as some ground support. They had also made attacks on RAF airfields and were about to take the opportunity to strike farther north, against Chittagong, Dohazari, Feni and Comilla. On the ground in April, the situation was becoming serious. British troops were fighting desperately in and around Donbaik, making gallant frontal attacks against heavily and well-defended Japanese fortified positions, but the enemy were well entrenched and the attackers suffered heavy losses.

Air combat continued, especially during March with 79, 135, 607 and 615 Squadrons all having successes. No.135 in particular got amongst Oscars on 5 March, claiming seven destroyed, six probably so and one damaged for no loss, during two engagements that day. Flight Lieutenant Jack Storey was credited with three. No.607 Squadron was also engaged this day, claiming one Oscar with three more damaged, but had one pilot wounded.

Another good day for 135 came on 27 March, against a force of Kawasaki Ki-48 Lily bombers. The squadron claimed seven shot down, with two probables and two damaged. Lee Hawkins, Norm Crawford, Jack Peabody, Hughie Dean 'Crafty' Fox and 'Army' Armstrong, got one each; Armstrong, Crawford and Bowes shared the seventh. No.79 Squadron also got into the action, adding another Lily destroyed and others damaged. Russ Bowes got this one, also sharing one of 135's victories. There were no losses for either 135 or 79.

However, there were losses on 9 April. Enemy aircraft headed for Chittagong as well as an independent Japanese fighter sweep. Blenheims and escorting Hurricanes had only just left this base on a raid, and 67 Squadron's planes were scrambled. As they did so, Oscars were already overhead and the enemy fighters came down on them as they were climbing desperately for height. Ken Hemingway, late of 17 Squadron, saw the diving fighters and yelled a warning over the radio, the Hurricanes having risen to only about 3,000 feet. The enemy were from the 64th Sentai, and spectators saw one Hurricane dive into the sea and another chasing an Oscar with two more on its tail. Bachmann and New Zealander Flying Officer W. Christianson were both killed, Bachmann's machine being later found crashed. He was twenty-five-years old and came from Norbury, Surrey. Two other Hurricanes were badly shot-up but returned safely.

No.67 Squadron was taken over by Squadron Leader J. S. Hart. John Hart had a long war as a fighter pilot. From New Brunswick, Canada, he had served with 54 and 602 Squadrons in the Battle of Britain. In 1941 he became a flight commander with

91 Squadron, before being posted out to Burma. For a time he flew with 9 Squadron, Indian Air Force, before taking over 67. In 1943 he left the Far East to fly with 112 Squadron in Italy in the last months of the war. His DFC was awarded in 1945.

* *

After almost three weeks of intensive operations by the Japanese air forces, the enemy scaled down their efforts on 11 April. All hope of taking Akyab in the minds of British leaders had been dashed, and their troops were in trouble, having been forced to retreat once again back to Rathedaung. They had had to extricate themselves from the enemy's encircling tactics and heavy casualties had occurred on both sides. By the middle of April the British and Indian forces had been forced back to positions around Maungdaw. The next monsoon would soon be approaching, but at least the Japanese air forces seemed to have been moved back once again, which allowed the RAF to improve its support missions for the men on the ground. There were now some Hurricane fighter-bomber squadrons operating, carrying 250lb or 500lb bombs beneath their wings. However, the Japanese airmen returned on 1 May 1943.

No.136 Squadron's first day at Chittagong, December 1942. By now some pith helmets have been replaced by steel helmets. Again a variety of garb is seen, from bare-chested, to shirts, to pullovers.

The Woodpeckers – 136 Squadron – decorated everything of theirs with a Woodpecker motif, thanks to the artistic skills of Pilot Officer Ian Adamson. Adamson, from Argentina, is seen here with his own personal insignia.

This is Ken Bunting's 136 Squadron Hurricane. He came from Yorkshire and had a Yorkshire terrier painted on his fighter.

Pilot Officer Chas Beale, 136 Squadron, as his Maori motif suggests, was from New Zealand.

Albert 'Bing' De Cruyenaere's Hurricane carried the Belgian flag and the name 'Leopold', the name of his king. He was RCAF and was killed in action on 15 March 1943.

Gordon Conway of 136 with his ground crew, Woodcroft and Martin. His fighter was HV952 R and was named 'Mignonetta'. It survived until July 1945 when it was 'struck off charge'.

Sergeant Steve 'Toot' deHorne, seated in Maurice Cuthbert's 'Stinky 1st'. Toot was allowed to grow a beard because of a skin complaint.

Joe Edwards, from Canada, depicted a sailing ship on his Hurricane, with 'Nova Scotia' written above it.

Viv Jacobs, another New Zealander in 136, had an eagle on his fighter (HW620), coded E. This machine was later flown by 1 Squadron IAF.

Even squadron vehicles carried the woodpecker emblem. Sergeant Bill Davis stands in front, with Vern Butler and Freddie Fortune by the door.

Flying Officer Viv Jacobs, 136 Squadron.

A woodpecker adorned Hurricane of 136 Squadron in flight. No unit code letters were carried by this time, just an aircraft identification letter.

The emblem on a 67 Squadron fighter. 'Deerhound' was also the squadron's call-sign in the air.

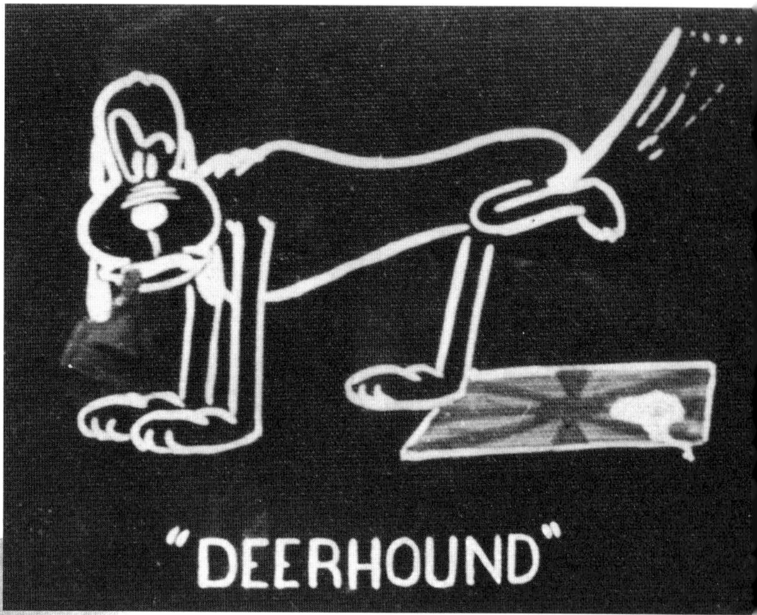

Flight Lieutenant P. J. T. Stephenson DFC. Paddy Stephenson was with 607 Squadron in the Battle of Britain and commanded it in Burma and was awarded the DFC. Afterwards he was on the personal staff of Lord Mountbatten.

Squadron Leader Barry Sutton DFC, commanding 135 Squadron.

The Hurricane of Sergeant F. W. T. Davis of 136 Squadron after combat on 10 December 1942 (BH142).

Bill Davis. Side arms were *de rigueur* for front-line fighter pilots in Burma. Later in 1943 Bill Davis managed to hit a Mitsubishi Ki-46 'Dinah', the first Hurricane pilot ever to score over one of these high-flying, fast, Japanese reconnaissance aircraft. It went down in a shallow dive, trailing smoke from one engine, and disappeared off the radar.

Flying Officer Jack Dawes of 607 Squadron had his Hurricane (BH139) damaged in air combat on 16 December 1942, operating out of Jessore, but got it back safely. Note the ambulance in the background.

The dispersal hut at Chittagong with petrol cans for quick refuelling and, therefore, a fire-extinguisher at the ready. April 1943.

Ken Perkin's (135 Squadron) wheels-up landing at Reindeer II airstrip south of Cox's Bazar on 7 April 1943. He had been in action with Oscar fighters, was shot up, and wounded in both legs.

Sergeant R. E. Windle, 135 Squadron. Bob arrived in September 1942 and in early 1943 he and his squadron were operating on the beach on the Burmese coast, code-named 'George', while the maintenance men were nearby at 'Hove' airstrip. He later flew Thunderbolts with this unit.

No. 607 Squadron had arrived and was at Alipore, awaiting a move to the Arakan front. This is B Flight: R. W. Bates, D. A. Blyth, A. M. Fraser, R. A. Hedderwick, W. G. Goold, H. L. Gill DFM, A. Murray, P. Macdonald, R. Smith, and Jack Dawes. Robin Hedderwick was the flight commander. Harry Gill was killed in action 17 January 1943, having won his DFM for operations from England, particularly during the Channel Dash. Pete MacDonald, son of a Member of Parliament in Brisbane, Australia, was killed on 11 March 1943.

Their sister squadron, 615, was at Feni. These three, in more formal dress, with long socks and pith helmets, take it easy on the airfield. They are: Graham Falconer, Denis Grestock and Al Horvath. Horvath was killed in a flying accident on 5 November 1942. Graham Falconer looks the picture of a bored fighter pilot waiting for something to happen.

A bad landing at Feni resulted in this 607 Squadron Hurricane digging its port wheel in, tipping the machine onto its nose. Note that this Hurricane is operating with eight .303 machine guns, whereas others in theatre were by then fitted with four 20mm cannon.

The pilots of 258 Squadron, having had a quiet time since seeing action over Ceylon, in April 1942, finally moved forward to Comilla, and, using a forward airstrip, began flying offensive sweeps down to Akyab. The picture is of Flying Officer D. B. F. Nicholls in his Hurricane looking very serious. Doug Nicholls would be awarded the DFC in 1944.

The new boss Woodpecker arrived in February 1943, Squadron Leader A. W. A. Bayne DFC. Alfie Bayne had flown with 17 Squadron during the Battle of Britain and received the DFC.

A pair of Hawker Hurricane IIs of 607 Squadron on patrol.

Three NCO pilots of 135 Squadron (with their young bearers). L to r: Sergeants J. Peabody, W. Brown and R. W. Edge. Jack Peabody claimed a Lily on 27 March, and an Oscar 'probable' on 31 March. Bill Brown claimed an Oscar on 5 March. Roy Edge, aged twenty from Croydon, Surrey, however, was shot down and killed on 31 March.

Pilots of 5 Squadron. When this unit first saw action in Burma it was flying Curtiss Mohawk fighters; it was then re-equipped with Hurricanes and finally Thunderbolts. Rear (l to r): Flight Lieutenant T. Trimble, -?-, Flight Lieutenant J. Lee, Flight Lieutenant R. R. Lawrence RCAF; Middle: Flying Officer B. Snowball RAAF, Flight Sergeant D. Parsons, Warrent Officer E. Worts, Flying Officer R. Mendizabal; Front: Flight Lieutenant D. J. T. Sharp RNZAF, Flight Lieutenant J. Rashleigh, Flying Officer A. S. Boyes, Flying Officer I. Baines, & Flying Officer G. Bailey. Denis Sharp had earlier flown with 258 Squadron, and later with 11 Squadron, winning the DFC. 'Smokey' Boyes had survived a collision with an Oscar, which crashed, on 19 January 1943, but was killed by ground fire on 24 April 1944. Flight Lieutenant Lawrence shot down a Lily on 7 October 1942, and later shared a Ki-21 Sally on 22 January 1943. John Rashleigh was later Squadron Leader Flying of 166 Wing.

CHAPTER FIVE

The Arrival of the Spitfire.

Fighting continued as the rains began, but on a reduced scale. The Japanese halted any form of assault northwards, and the British forces dug in again on the original line by the Mayu peninsula. The final phase of the Arakan fight had seen the Japanese air forces attempting to attack RAF airfields, in order to stop operations against their forward troops.

Both sides were flying light bombing missions, and on occasion raiding forces would meet, and the fighters started to mix it with the opposition. By this time other RAF fighter squadrons were operating over the Arakan front. No.146 was at Feni and then Comilla, with detachments at Chittagong. Squadron Leader G. R. T. Williams was OC. No.67 Squadron was also at Chittagong now, commanded by Squadron Leader D. W. A. Stones DFC*, veteran of France, the Battle of Britain and Malta. He had been a supernumerary until Squadron Leader J. H. Bachmann was killed in action against Japanese fighters on 9 April 1943. At Ramu, with detachments on three forward airstrips, Hay, Lyons and Ritz, 79 Squadron was now commanded by Squadron Leader D. O. Cunliffe. Don Stones was wounded on 15 May during a strafing attack on a Japanese airfield at Kamgaung, a satellite of Meiktila in Central Burma, but he brought his Hurricane home. This action was also the last for Ken Hemingway as he was to be rested.

The RAF lost an exceptional fighter pilot on 21 May, in a fight with the 64th Sentai. Flight Lieutenant R. R. H. Bowes DFC of 79 Squadron was lost in air combat, along with New Zealander Sergeant Ken Burchard, aged twenty from Hawke's Bay. The Japanese had launched a massive fighter sweep over Cox's Bazar, with Oscars of the 50th and 64th Sentais. No.67 scrambled their fighters into a cloudy sky and Burchard, on his first operational sortie, breaking from a cloud, ran slap into about a dozen Oscars and didn't stand a chance. Russ Bowes simply failed to return. He had just received his promotion to flight lieutenant and been awarded the DFC. Bowes, from Australia, had accounted for at least five Japanese aircraft with others damaged.

The Woodpecker Squadron got in amongst Japanese bombers on 22 May, resulting in claims for three Kawasaki Ki-48 bombers and two Oscars. Three others of each type were also marked as probables or damaged while 67 Squadron got another bomber with two more and a fighter damaged. The 136 Squadron claimants were Eric Brown, Ian Adamson, Bob Stout, Gordon Conway and Freddie Fortune. Viv Jacobs, McDonald and Johnnie Rudling accounted for the damaged ones. This squadron was in action again on 29 May: Paddy Kearon shot down a Lily, Jim Gillies DFM another and an Oscar, Gordon Conway got an Oscar, with Stout and Rudling again claiming Oscars as damaged. In both actions, only one 136 Squadron was lost on the 22nd (Rudling, but he was not injured despite being forced to take to his parachute), while on the 29th one was damaged (Kearon's). The Woodpeckers were a trifle over-optimistic with their claims, but being the last major air fight before the monsoon, the enemy knew they had been in a battle.

* *

Both sides attempted to hold each other at bay during the following weeks, RAF bombers and fighters flying as weather permitted during the monsoon period. At this time several Blenheim squadrons were withdrawn and re-equipped with Hurricanes for fighter-bomber operations. A number of the fighter squadrons again withdrew towards India where more permanent airfields were preferred to the jungle strips with their mud and high winds.

The Japanese were still determined to get into India, and were now planning a two pronged thrust after the monsoon. First was to be another push up through the Arakan, while another force would attempt to push back the British farther west and north, into the Chin Hills, and capture the Imphal Valley area from a more easterly direction. If successful, this would allow them to head north through the valley, where, sixty miles farther on was Kohima. Once Kohima was taken, the way was open to Dimapur, where the railway led directly into north-east India.

Meantime, the Spitfire had finally arrived in India. With the demands of other fronts for this supreme fighter aeroplane, such as Malta and North Africa, even Australia,

India/Burma was again at the end of the queue. Politics, too, played a part, for earlier one senior RAF commander had refused Spitfires, believing the Hurricane to be better in this theatre due to their ruggedness on rough airstrips. However, Spitfires began to be shipped in and, in September 1943, 607 Squadron became the first unit to start converting to them from their old Hurricanes. The first arrived by sea at Karachi in crates where they were assembled and tested, then pilots were sent across India to collect them and fly them back to Alipore.

The initial problem was to find pilots who had Spitfire experience who could collect the aircraft that were starting to be made ready in Karachi. The first six chosen were from 607 and 615 Squadrons, Squadron Leader P. J. T. Stephenson DFC, Flying Officer Colin Doudy, Flying Officer G. W. Andrews, Flying Officer A. F. C. Valentine, Flying Officer Dennis Grestock and Flight Sergeant H. B. Chandler. The pilots flew to Karachi in the Empire flying-boat *Caledonian* on 4 September 1943. Once there they tested the Spitfires at the Test and Despatch Flight airfield and on the 14th flew them back. Four days later Stephenson and the others returned for a second batch. The flight plan to cross India was Karachi to Jodhpur, Jodhpur to Allahabad, Allahabad to Calcutta, a total of 1,500 miles in one day. As one pilot noted, 'Was my bottom sore'. As other pilots gained experience on the new Spitfires, so they too were flown to Karachi to collect others.

The RAF in Burma desperately needed a fighter better than the Hurricane in order to retain air superiority over the battle areas by combating the Oscars. It was planned to increase the number of transport aircraft for forthcoming battles and they would need a clear sky and protection if they were to be allowed to carry out their supply dropping sorties without interference. These supply aircraft were American Douglas C-47 Dakotas, one of the most reliable aircraft in this type of work. During the Second World War they were used in every theatre and battle area. Burma offered little in the way of open fighting areas; almost everything had to be achieved through jungle terrain, so the best way of supporting troops on the ground was by parachute air drop. Dakotas could carry twenty-eight paratroopers, but it was their ability to fly in around 8,000 pounds of food and ammunition that made them so essential.

The Spitfires that began to arrive were Mark Vs with tropical air filters, later followed by Mark VIIIs. Tropical filters had been essential for work in the North African deserts and it seemed sensible to have them on the dusty airstrips of Burma. The Hurricanes had used them too. The Spitfires carried two 20mm cannon and four .303

machine guns, better hitting power than Hurricane Mk I, which had eight .303s. The Hurricane Mk IIC had four 20mm cannon, of course, although some pilots flew with just two in order to improve manoeuvrability against the nimble Oscars. Cannon-armed Hurricanes were mostly used for ground attack sorties.

Flight Lieutenant Guy Hogan's 79 Squadron Hurricane 'X' following his crash-landing after a fight with enemy bombers and fighters when they raided Chittagong on 15 December 1942. Note the bullet holes in the top of the engine cowling.

Every little helps, or is it too many cooks? No. 135 ground crew service a Hurricane on a forward airstrip. Still using pith helmets, and with socks and rubber boots, it must have been the wet season.

Operating from the forward airstrip called 'Ritz' (Maungdaw 1), 135 Squadron had a number of air battles in early 1943. Flight Lieutenant L. C. C. Hawkins with his Hurricane. Note long-range fuel tank. Written on the side of the aircraft in chalk is: 'ACL fitted, Do Not Rewire'. Hawkins shot down a Lily on 27 March 1943, and damaged two more.

135 Squadron pilots (l to r): W. H. F. Dean (NZ), A. M. Morrison, 'Hap' Armstrong, Jim McIvor and Lee Hawkins. Hughie Dean was killed in action on 31 March 1943, Sandy Morrison was killed in action on 14 March 1943.

Jack Peabody of 135 Squadron was another victorious pilot in early 1943. A Lily on 27 March and an Oscar 'probable' on the 31st.

Lee Hawkins, Jack Storey, Eric Batchelor and Ray Prince, 135 Squadron. Australian Jack Storey was one of the first pilots to arrive in Rangoon and remained with the squadron until August 1943, claiming eight victories and being awarded the DFC. Tragically, Prince was shot down by an RAF fighter by mistake on 11 March 1943, while on an air test from Hove.

Two pals in 136 Squadron, D. F. 'Freddie' Pickard from Sydenham, South London, aged twenty-two, and D. E. 'Fuggy' Fuge from Eastbourne, Sussex. Pickard was lost in action on 15 March 1943, and Fuge, another early arrival into Rangoon in early 1942, was killed in air combat on 15 January 1944.

Japanese Kawasaki Ki-48 (Lily) bomber caught on a Hurricane's camera gun film.

Flight Lieutenant Eric 'Bojo' Brown of 136 Squadron shot down a Lily on 22 May near Chittagong. Brownie came from Blackburn, Lancashire, and was, at thirty-five, Daddy Woodpecker. His DFC was gazetted in February 1944.

Gordon Conway from North London, 136 Squadron. Born in March 1923 he lied about his age to join the RAF, and so was only just twenty when in action on 22 and 29 May 1943. He would receive the DFC before the end of the year.

Paddy Kearon's Hurricane after the fight on 29 May 1943 in which he was wounded but claimed a bomber.

Paddy Kearon and Pete Kennedy, 136 Squadron. Kennedy was shot down on 28 February 1943 and baled out. He was fortunate to survive as he hit the ground moments after his parachute deployed. He was to die in combat on 20 January 1944. Kearon was killed in a similar fashion on 5 February.

Flight Lieutenant Russ Bowes DFC, aged twenty-seven, from Springfield, South Australia, was lost in action on 29 May 1943. He had claimed five enemy aircraft shot down and shared in another.

Flight Lieutenant Ken Clark RCAF of 607 Squadron with his Spitfire and personal crest, designed around a Canadian maple leaf. Clark shared an Oscar on 24 December 1942, and damaged another. He claimed another as a 'probable' on 5 March, damaging yet another ten days later.

Flying Officer Colin Doudy RAAF, with his personalised 607 Squadron Spitfire (LZ975). His motif shows a Scottish thistle and the name 'Sheena II'. The real Sheena, who came from Scotland, later became his wife. Doudy had been one of the pilots to ferry Spitfires across India. He shot down an Oscar on 17 January 1943, but it was a year before he got another, on 15 January 1944, plus a damaged. On 21 February he damaged three more.

In front of a 136 Squadron Spitfire, with long-range tanks, are Flight Lieutenant Eric Brown, Squadron Leader Noel Constantine, Flight Lieutenant Joe Edwards RCAF and Flying Officer L. H. 'Dopey' LeCraw RCAF. LeCraw had been shot down into the sea in 1942 and wounded in the face, but returned. Eric Brown had also suffered a shoot down and parachute descent from a Hurricane. Noel Constantine was 136's new CO, having taken over from Alfie Bayne in June 1943. He had earlier commanded 273 Squadron on Ceylon.

The tropicalised Spitfire V, as used in the North African desert campaign, arrives in India. It would soon make its mark in the skies over Burma.

CHAPTER SIX

Calcutta, Second Arakan, and Operation BROADWAY.

One of the first things the new Spitfires demonstrated was their ability to catch the high-flying, fast Mitsubishi Ki-46 reconnaissance aircraft, known more familiarly to the RAF pilots as Dinah. Often, incursions by these aircraft were a precursor to a Japanese air attack. No.615 Squadron, now under the command of Squadron Leader R. H. Holland DFC, was operational at Chittagong. Bob Holland was yet another experienced former Battle of Britain veteran, who in fact was born in Ceylon and had been a Cranwell cadet. He had flown with 92 Squadron over Dunkirk and throughout the Battle of Britain, and had then flown with 91 'Jim Crow' Squadron in 1941. Having brought 615 Squadron to India in 1942, he had then commanded 607 Squadron for a while, but was now back leading 615.

In November 1943, just before the squadron moved into Feni, it had the good fortune to knock down three Dinahs in comparatively quick succession. On 8 November, Flight Lieutenant P. G. Louis DFC DFM, in company with Flying Officer S. L. E. Weggery RNZAF, were scrambled at 0745 am, under GCI control and spotted the recce machine at 25,000 feet, turning over Chittagong town. This was slightly below them so they both dived to the attack, gaining speed for the expected chase. Paul Louis fired first, his ASI reading 250mph. The enemy pilot quickly turned into the sun and then headed south, thinking no doubt that, as in the past, he would easily out-distance the RAF fighters. Over Dohazari, Louis had got close enough to the Dinah to open fire again, then closed right in to fifty yards. The Japanese aircraft's starboard engine burst into flame, and a third attack punched holes in the starboard wing which began to stream petrol vapour. Weggery now attacked, his de Wilde ammunition starting to explode all over the Dinah, as it began to dive. Pieces began to be blasted from it and then the whole machine became a ball of fire and its starboard wing ripped off. What was left crashed to the ground north-east of Chiringa. This was the first 'confirmed' victory by Spitfires on the Burma front.

On 10 November Flight Sergeant A. R. Hyde shot down a second Dinah and then on 16th, Flying Officer K. F. Gannon and Flight Sergeant I. Dickson bagged a third. On Boxing Day, 26 December, Flying Officer R. E. J. MacDonald and Flight Sergeant R. O. Patterson of 152 Squadron, shot down another Dinah. The Japanese were starting to be blinded through lack of intelligence from their recce aircraft. This was emphasised on 16 January 1944, Louis and Weggery shooting down another Dinah while, on 5 February, Flying Officer L. G. Coons and Sergeant J. B. Neville of 607 Squadron, shared yet another.

On 15 November 1943, the RAF fighter squadrons on the India/Burma front were as follows:

No.221 Fighter Group, Calcutta			
No.79 Sqn	Alipore	Hurricane IIc	S/Ldr C. A. Jones
No.136 Sqn	Baigachi	Spitfire Vc	S/Ldr A. N. Constantine
No.607 Sqn	Alipore	Spitfire Vc	S/Ldr P. J. T. Stephenson DFC
No.224 Fighter Group, Chittagong			
No.28 Sqn	Cox's Bazar	Hurricane IIb	S/Ldr H. G. F. Larsen
(Detachment only)			
No.165 Fighter Wing, Ramu			
No.258 Sqn	Dohazari	Hurricane IIb	S/Ldr F. G. Land
No.166 Fighter Wing, Chittagong			
No.67 Sqn	Chittagong	Hurricane IIc	S/Ldr T. C. Parker
No.261 Sqn	Chiringa	Hurricane IIc	S/Ldr C. F. Counter
No.615 Sqn	Chittagong	Spitfire Vc	S/Ldr R. H. Holland DFC
No.185 Fighter Wing, Feni			
No.11 Sqn	Lalmai	Hurricane IIc	S/Ldr S. C. Norris DFC
No.60 Sqn	Agartala	Hurricane IIc	S/Ldr R. C. Lindsell RCAF
No.146 Sqn	Comilla	Hurricane IIc	S/Ldr L. M. O'Leary AFC

* *

The Indian city of Calcutta was an important centre for transport, especially for war materials. The Japanese were well aware of its importance and were keen to disrupt the flow of arms and ammunition as well as unnerve the civilian population. With the RAF occupied elsewhere, including the three new Spitfire squadrons, the Japanese 5th Air Division decided to attack on 5 December 1943. It was to be an historic occasion, for quite apart from twenty-seven Army 97 bombers (Sally), escorted by over a hundred Oscars, and supported by others that had flown across from China and up from Sumatra, the Japanese Navy would be in on it. The Navy airmen would mount a second wave, of nine Mitsubishi G4M 'Betty' bombers, escorted by Zeros, and timed to hit Calcutta as the defending RAF fighters were landing to refuel and re-arm from the first engagement. It was the first time both Army and Navy aircraft had co-operated in an air attack on an Allied target. Japanese air reconnaissance had noted over sixty ships in the harbour and the King George V docks; it was too good a target to ignore.

Calcutta was defended by No. 293 Wing. Although mainly used as a transit wing, it had three Hurricane squadrons, 67 at Alipore, 146 at Bagaichi, having moved in just the day before, and 79 Squadron which had flown into Alipore on the morning of the 5th from Chittagong. There was a Beaufighter squadron too, 176, also at Bagaichi, which also had Hurricanes, experimentally fitted with AI (Airborne Radar) that necessitated their armour being removed. The AI did not prove a success and, on the Calcutta raid, they were used as ordinary day-fighters.

Early on the 5th British radar picked up a Japanese reconnaissance plane, a sure sign that trouble was coming. At around 0930 radar began picking up bogies over the Bay of Bengal. Within minutes Spitfires began to be scrambled from the Chittagong area – 136, 607 and 615 Squadrons, plus Hurricanes from 60, 258 and 261. By this time the estimated force of thirty-plus enemy aircraft was some seventy miles west-north-west of Akyab, way out over the bay, each minute pulling away from most of the interceptors. In the final analysis only 136 and 258 were able to intercept.

Radar at Calcutta could now see the approaching hostiles and scrambled 146's experimental Hurricanes. Later 67 Squadron was also sent aloft, joining up with nine Hurricanes of 146. Several air battles ensued with each side claiming victories. Eric Brown of 136 downed a Sally, as did 'Ginger' Hickes of 258 Squadron. No.67 claimed one Oscar with four more damaged, while 146 probably got another and 261 Squadron claimed another as probably destroyed and a 'Hamp' (Zero) damaged.

The Japanese did better. Eric Brown was hit and force landed on a sandbank. Art Brown of 258 was killed and 67 Squadron lost one pilot and had two more Hurricanes damaged. No.146 lost one and had three damaged, but all four pilots survived. No.261 had one aircraft damaged but 176 had four casualties, three Hurricanes lost with two pilots killed and a fourth machine damaged. Among their losses was Flying Officer A. M. O. Pring DFM. Maurice Pring was ordinarily a Beaufighter pilot who had gained several night-fighter victories in the Middle East and over Malta. On the night of 15/16 January 1943 he and his navigator/radar operator had downed three Sally bombers in an earlier Calcutta raid.

As the second wave was spotted, every available aircraft was sent up, including four Beaufighters of 176, plus five of their AI Hurricanes. It was in this fight that Pring was shot down. Al Corston, RCAF, of native Indian descent, found the second wave, or rather it found him. He realised he was not up against Oscars and later learned they were indeed Navy Zero fighters. As luck would have it his radio packed up and he could hear nothing of the battle or where the enemy could be located. Glancing in his rear-view mirror he saw two radial-engined fighters behind, getting ready to clobber him. He had just begun to think all this was just a practice scramble! He got away fast.

Some damage was done to the target, but the main damage was to Indian morale and once again there followed a mass exodus from the city with the resultant slow-down of supplies to the battle fronts as dock and harbour labourers headed out of town.

* *

With both the Allies and the Japanese poised again for a confrontation along the Bengal Coast as the monsoon abated, the Spitfire would hopefully begin to make its presence felt against the Japanese Army Air Force. As was usual, the latter generally kept well out of the way and only moved aircraft to forward airfields when they planned a raid.

The Japanese were once more confident of success and, to meet such an assault, the British 5th Division had taken over part of the 7th Division's front line, freeing the 7th to operate again against Buthidaung and along the eastern side of the Mayu. In preparation, the British pioneers had developed a jungle track through the

Ngakyedauk Pass into a proper military road, and could move tanks and medium artillery forward. However, before anything could really start to happen, intelligence suggested the Japanese were once again about to launch an offensive.

What was going to change this time was that rather than fight, and retreat, the British soldiers were told to stand their ground, dig in, and resist. By this time the RAF had got its supply act together, and the commanders promised that ground troops would be supplied from the air by Dakota parachute drops. The Japanese soldier, as ever, was given a gun, ammunition and some rice, and ordered forward into the attack. The Japanese had no real method of resupply, their practice having always been to re-supply themselves on the march with captured materials, especially of food. This time, while they well might encircle, they would fail to force a retreat.

Before this all began, the RAF fighter pilots had several dogfights with Japanese aircraft, notably on Boxing Day, 26 December. It began with 152 Squadron shooting down a Japanese recce machine. No.152, along with 81 Squadron, were newly arrived in India and brought the Spitfire squadron numbers to five. Both squadrons had been in action in the Middle East and were flying the improved Spitfire Mk VIIIs. No.152 was commanded by Squadron Leader M. R. B. Ingram DFC, 81 by Squadron Leader W. M. Whitamore DFC.

Sally bombers and escorting Oscars headed for Chittagong, a total of twenty-one bombers and seventy-eight Oscars. Not for the first time radar gave a poor interpretation of what was going on. Two pilots of 615 Squadron were scrambled to intercept what was deemed a lone raider but once in the air the size of the plot kept increasing. As it reached forty-plus the rest of 615 were ordered up. Then the two lone pilots, Flying Officer G. W. Andrews and fellow Australian Flight Sergeant H. B. Chandler, ran into the enemy formation. They plunged into them, Bill Andrews firing into one Oscar at close range and it fell away, later to be found crashed and full of holes. He followed this up by shooting down a bomber, and Chan Chandler knocked down two bombers. Bill also damaged another Sally.

Pilots of 136 Squadron were also sent up but only two succeeded in locating the raiders. Flight Sergeant R. W. Cross shot down two fighters while Pilot Officer J. D. Rudling got a Sally. In fact, his attack came so close he actually hit the bomber's tail with the underside of his Spitfire. Later a Japanese flag from this bomber was sent to the squadron as a souvenir. All this was achieved with just one loss, as twenty-year-old Sergeant Donald L. Wright RCAF, from Saskatoon, of 615, did not get home and his machine was later found north of Chittagong, apparently jumped by Japanese fighters.

Five days later the Japanese tried again, and the Woodpeckers gave them a bloody nose. Bob Cross, from Suffolk, already had considerable combat experience since the beginning of the year, his victory tally standing at five with another probable and two damaged. He had an uncanny knack of predicting when the Japanese would mount an attack, and even went so far as to write the date on the flight blackboard. He was invariably right and even swopped places with other pilots on readiness, if necessary, so that he would be on call when the alert sounded.

On the 31st the Japanese went for some navy minelayers off St Martin's Island, to the south of the Naf river estuary; these vessels had earlier bombarded Ramree Island. As breakfast arrived from the mess tent at 136's dispersal, the order came to scramble. Constantine, Conway and Eric Brown led three four-man sections and, over the bay, spotted the bombers heading for the ships. In the attack the Woodpeckers claimed eight Sally bombers shot down, three others probably destroyed and five damaged, plus three Oscars with four more damaged. Another two were seen to collide in the battle. No.136 suffered no loss. Conway got two bombers and an Oscar, plus an Oscar probable, and a Sally damaged. Bob Cross got one Sally, one Oscar and two bombers damaged. Denis Garvan claimed a Sally, another probably destroyed and two Oscars damaged. Vern Butler claimed three bombers in each category. Other pilots shared the rest. So ended 1943.

At the start of 1944, there were six Spitfire squadrons operational, based as follows:

No.165 Wing			
No.136 Sqn	Ramu	Spitfire Vc	S/Ldr A. N. Constantine
No.607 Sqn	Ramu	Spitfire Vc	S/Ldr P. J. T. Stephenson DFC
No.166 Wing			
No.615 Sqn	Dohazari	Spitfire Vc	S/Ldr R. H. Holland DFC
No.293 Wing			
No.152 Sqn	Baigachi	Spitfire VIII	S/Ldr M. R. B. Ingram DFC
No.155 Sqn	Alipore	Spitfire VIII	S/Ldr D. Winton DFC
Imphal Valley			
No.81 Sqn	Tulihal	Spitfire VIII	S/Ldr W. M. Whitamore DFC

January 1944 began with more air combats over the Arakan coast, 136 and 607 Squadrons claiming several hostile aircraft shot down during January and this would continue into February, with the start of the Japanese offensive, while 81 Squadron also began to achieve successes. The RAF pilots began to identify Hamps among the Oscars but, rather than being Navy Zero types, these were undoubtedly Ki-43 Oscar Mark IIs. However, as the expected enemy thrust north towards Chittangong started, it caught the British a little off guard. One force of Japanese, with some skill, managed to penetrate the eastern flank of the 7th Indian Division, approaching through some dense jungle and capturing Taung Bazar before being discovered. Another Japanese force attacked the British front line north and northwest of Buthidaung.

After taking Taung Bazar, this force turned to the south-west for the strategic Ngakyedauk Pass. Immediately General Bill Slim, commander of the newly-created Fourteenth Army in Burma began moves to thwart these attacks. In the air the Japanese were continuing their offensive action, trying to wrest air supremacy over the battle areas.

On the ground, despite the attempt at encirclement by the Japanese, the British troops, as ordered, stayed put and dug in. What developed became known as the Battle of the Admin Box, because men of all ranks and all duties, whether it be cooks, soldiers or administrative personnel, took up arms and defended the perimeter, while RAF transport aircraft, as promised, flew in parachute supply drops to keep the defenders supplied with food and ammunition. The battle continued for some time, but the Japanese soon realised that something had changed, and the enemy were not 'playing the game' and retreating. For their part, their own food and ammunition stocks were rapidly diminishing.

* *

Farther inland from the Bengal coast, other operations were being planned. In the far north of Burma, the American General, 'Vinegar Joe' Stilwell, who had been fighting with the Chinese under Chiang Kai-shek, and now Deputy Supreme Allied Commander, under Lord Mountbatten, opened his long-prepared offensive to take the Japanese base at Myitkyina, in December 1943.

Farther south, there had been one unusual event back in February 1943, that saw a force of British soldiers, who became known as the Chindits, under General Orde Wingate, cross the Chindwin river and, in March, the Irrawaddy. Their task was to destroy bridges, Japanese bases and communication routes, and they had some limited success before being forced to withdraw.

In early 1944 Wingate planned another, larger operation, but this time, rather than walking in, his much larger force would be airlifted deep behind Japanese lines (some 200 miles), although one brigade did march in, and from there would again attack the Japanese. Also this time, the Chindits would have a squadron of Spitfires operating with them in the jungle; this was 81 Squadron.

Operation THURSDAY began on 5 March 1944, with a large force of transport aircraft, RAF and USAAF, fifty-four of which towed troop-laden gliders. Landing areas had been prepared, codenamed 'Piccadilly', 'Broadway' and 'Chowringhee', and into them went the Chindit force. Squadron Leader 'Babe' Whitamore's 81 Squadron provided a section of Spitfires for local defence, and they flew in on the 10th. By this time the place was littered with abandoned and crashed gliders and, virtually every day, transport aircraft were heading in and out, parachuting down supplies, or landing to take out the wounded.

Six Spitfires were flown in, one being damaged almost immediately and used for spares. Two of the detachment were Middle East veterans, friends Alan Peart, from New Zealand, and Larry Cronin, an Australian. As a base it was impossible to defend against air attack for, other than a very basic radar set, which was never going to be any good as an early warning system, the Japanese bases were near at hand. Indeed, when enemy fighters did attack, 81 Squadron was caught out and, despite becoming airborne, lost one pilot shot down into the jungle soon after getting into the air. The Spitfires were joined a few days later by some American P-51 fighters but it was far too dangerous to operate from here. After a week the Spitfires were withdrawn but they had suffered losses. Whitamore had been killed and another pilot had died in his cockpit as strafing Japanese fighters came over. It had been a costly exercise.

Three 615 Squadron pilots involved in the shooting down of three Ki-46 Dinah reconnaissance aircraft over the Arakan, Flight Sergeant A. R. 'Bill' Hyde, Flight Lieutenant Paul Louis DFC DFM, and Flying Officer S. L. E. Weggery RNZAF.

'Weg' Weggery's Spitfire (MA349) with its two Japanese victory flags painted on the fuselage and the name 'Verna June II' by the cockpit. It was coded KW-D and had a New Zealand fern leaf painted beneath the exhaust stacks. The three airmen are Messrs Barke, Baker and Bagnell, his rigger, armourer and fitter.

Flight Lieutenant Kevin Gannon, 615 Squadron, and his Spitfire. The insignia is a small dog that has just defecated on a Japanese flag, with the name 'Snifter' written above it. A former police cadet from Queensland, Australia, he held temporary command of 615 in August and September 1944.

Flight Lieutenant Derrick Brocklehurst led the AI-equipped Hurricanes of 176 Squadron against Japanese raiders going for Calcutta on 5 December 1943. They had expected to be vectored on to a lone Japanese reconnaissance aeroplane but suddenly ran into a gaggle of Zero fighters, much to their surprise.

Pilot Officer Andy Whyte RCAF, another in an AI Hurricane of 176 Squadron. He was shot down by a Navy Zero and it took two days for him to return to base.

Sergeant Ed Griffiths, a 146 Squadron pilot in action above Calcutta. With others on this scramble he had been to a party the previous night before flying to Baigachi. They were making their way to their new quarters when the order to take off came. Then it was cancelled, but soon they were ordered off again, which was why they were well below the Japanese raiders. Griffiths dived away and, looking back up, all he could see were Japanese fighters. Suffering a broken con-rod, he was forced to make a crash-landing and came home by train.

Pilot Officer Peter 'Ginger' Hickes of 258 Squadron. He attacked and shot down a Sally before being engaged by an Oscar but managed to evade it and escape. Hickes was killed in a mid-air collision two weeks later, on 19 December.

Warrant Officer Al Corston RCAF, 67 Squadron (with feathered friends). Al, of native red Indian descent, saw action over Calcutta, had a crack at an Oscar, and was so close he didn't know how he had missed.

Pilots of 615 Squadron, (l to r): Bill 'Mac' McMasters, Bill Andrews, F. S. Hunt RNZAF, Chan Chandler, I. Dickson, F. A. Fox and Ray 'Doc' Maddocks. Andrews and Chandler were successful on 26 December 1943. McMasters, Hunt and twenty-two-year-old Maddocks, from Sheffield, did not survive Burma.

Johnny Rudling DFM RNZAF of 136 Squadron got a Sally on 26 December 1943. A Maori, Rudling had received the DFM in November and would soon be given a commission. He was killed over Meiktila airfield in April 1944, helping to save a brother pilot.

Three pilots holding a Japanese flag, a souvenir from one of the Sally bombers shot down on 31 December: R. J. Clarke RNZAF, C. J. Moorhouse and Ken Bunting.

Another 'line-shoot' pose on 31 December 1943. Johnnie Rudling does the acting to the Intelligence Officer, while Bob Cross enjoys the antics. Cross had bagged one bomber and one fighter in the action, and damaged two more of the bombers. Note Rudling's side-arm and ammunition belt.

Three pilots of 136 Squadron (l to r): Johnnie Rudling DFM, D. E. W. Garvan RAAF and F. E. Wilding. Denis Garvan had been successful on 31 December 1943, claiming one Sally destroyed, one probably destroyed and two Oscars damaged. On 15 January 1944 he shot down two fighters, probably another and damaged a fourth. Five days later, he brought his score to 4-2-4, although he was wounded in this engagement. Frank Wilding destroyed a fighter and probably one more in two sorties on the 15th.

Squadron Leader W. M. Whitamore DFC, CO of 81 Squadron, who led a flight of Spitfires into 'Broadway' in order to operate with the Chindits. He was killed in action there on 17 March 1944.

Flying Officer A. McG. Peart RNZAF of 81 Squadron also operated from 'Broadway' and claimed victories from there. Alan Peart had seen considerable action with 81 in North Africa in 1942-43. His Spitfire was the only one not to be destroyed during this dangerous operation. After the subsequent Imphal battle he received the DFC, bringing his overall score to 6-1-9.

Flying Officer L. F. M. Cronin RAAF, was another member of 81 Squadron's 'Broadway' detachment. He, too, had considerable North African combat experience and brought his score to five destroyed on 13 March 1944. He also received the DFC. The marking of a Japanese flag on the 'ace of spades' insignia denotes his victory over a Dinah recce plane on 6 March 1944.

CHAPTER SEVEN
The Defence of Imphal and Kohima

Despite the Chindits making a nuisance of themselves to the enemy in central Burma, the Japanese were not deflected from their goal of getting into India. With their second attempt at moving north through the Arakan thwarted by the British policy of not retreating on the ground, and also trying to keep operating as best they could through the monsoon period, they now headed into the Chin Hills of northern Burma.

In their way was the mighty Imphal Valley, through which ran a main road north to Kohima, then Dimapur. If these could be captured, the gateway to India was open, and with it the Bengal and Assam railway line. However, there was considerable Allied defence in the valley, especially once the British, seeing the danger, moved 5th Indian Division into the area. This was done almost overnight with a massive airlift of men, and supplies, all courtesy of the RAF and USAAF transport aircraft and their crews. With 5th Division in place, 7th then followed.

Also in the valley were no fewer than six airfields, although airstrips might just as easily be the term. These were: Imphal Main, Palel, Wangjing, Tulihal, Kangla and Sapam. However, only Tulihal and Palel were deemed to be all-weather strips. The British IV Corps, under General G. A. P. Scoones CSI DSO OBE MC, ran the defence in the valley, with its HQ just to the north of Imphal town, close to the main airfield. At his disposal, Scoones had three divisions and one tank brigade. Kohima was just over sixty miles to the north with Silchar ninety miles due west. The main road headed into the valley from Tamu, situated sixteen miles to the south-east. Moving into the locality, the Japanese took Tamu, which had an airstrip, and from there they planned to infiltrate north into the valley as well as curving north and west towards Kohima.

As suggested by its name, the Imphal Valley was more or less surrounded by hills. Once the Japanese advanced this far north, they occupied these hills, from where they could look down to the valley floor and see the airfields. British Army units naturally had defensive positions reasonably well covered, but once in situ they could not stop Japanese soldiers infiltrating into the valley at night, but they always retreated back into the hills by dawn. Spitfires flew into the airfields to help the defence, and especially to give air cover to the air supply drops, bringing in food and ammunition to the defenders. So long as the valley and its main through road were not lost, any large assault upon Kohima was stopped from that direction. The Japanese, of course, attacked Kohima over the hills and through the jungle, but without a road, heavy equipment, such as tanks and heavy artillery, could not be brought in.

However, once Japanese troops had begun to attack Kohima through the Chin Hills, it became a very difficult position to hold and defend. Although the Japanese had cut the main road north out of Imphal at Milestone 109, their troops were unable to progress through Imphal from the south, and join up with their forces around Kohima. Equally, any British help for the Kohima defenders north from Imphal by road was also blocked.

It was fortunate that Operation THURSDAY was undertaken when it had been, for once the valley was surrounded, transport aircraft that had flown Wingate's 10,000 men into Broadway (and the other landing areas, Piccadilly and Chowringhee) would not have been able to use those valley airfields in great numbers for this massive operation. Fortunately, as the siege progressed, RAF and USAAF C-47s were able to use Imphal Main and Tulihal, provided they slipped in, unloaded and got off quickly. Supply aircraft flying in from here, or from Dergaon, Agartala, Sylhet, etc., to the west, were able to give superb aid to the men fighting desperately at Kohima.

When the Spitfire squadrons moved in, due to the very nature of the siege-like conditions, they had to create what were called 'boxes'. In other words, each night pilots and ground personnel withdrew into underground bunkers, almost like First World War trench systems, whilst wheeling the aircraft into close proximity for protection. These boxes had trip-wires around them to catch out any enemy soldiers who edged too close, and guard duties were undertaken by both air and ground personnel. Gurkha soldiers helped with the defences, even sending out nocturnal patrols in the hope of locating Japanese soldiers wandering about. Several airmen later recollected that some patrols came back gleefully showing the RAF men small items cut from Japanese soldiers' anatomies, which they kept in bloodsoaked matchboxes.

The Woodpecker Squadron (136) had flown in to Sapam and then to Wangjing, although its transport, such as petrol bowsers, petrol drums and trucks, had to be driven from the Arakan, which took ten days along jungle tracks and dirt roads. No.607 Squadron moved into Wangjing, 615 into Palel and 81 into Tulihul while 152 Squadron went initially to Palel, and then to Imphal Main.

There were still several Hurricane squadrons operating, although most had by this time become fighter-bomber units. Those operating during the Imphal battle, all part of No.229 Group RAF, were 5, 11, 20, 28, 34, 42, 60, 113, 123, plus 1 and 9 Indian Air Force Squadrons. These were occasionally based in the valley, and sometimes had aircraft re-arm and refuel there during daylight. Their task was to bomb, strafe and generally harass Japanese troops, positions, bunkers, supply routes and encampments. Bombing makeshift bridges across streams and sunken roads helped delay supplies to front-line troops from Tamu, and especially those in the hills surrounding Kohima.

The importance of Kohima was due to its being a junction for four main routes in an almost trackless country. In peacetime it had been a hill station for Assam and during the early stages of the war was used as a hospital area for IV Corps. It is 5,000 feet above sea level and, at this time of the year, nights are very cold. Nearby high ground enabled Japanese light artillery to set up and begin firing into the small perimeter held by the defenders, who occupied an area of defence, on 5 April, of 1,100 yards by 700 yards by 950 yards. The garrison comprised of around 3,000 men. Once again they were promised supplies by air-drop, which the C-47s carried out.

The following RAF fighter squadrons operated within 221 Group during the siege, between March and July 1944:

No.5 Sqn	Lanka	Hurricane IIc	S/Ldr G. J. C. Hogan DFC
No.11 Sqn	Lanka	Hurricane IIc	S/Ldr D. J. T. Sharp DFC
No.20 Sqn	Chiringa	Hurricane IId	S/Ldr A. B. Miller DFC
No.28 Sqn	Jorhat	Hurricane IIc	S/Ldr H. G. F. Larsen DFC
No.34 Sqn	Dergaon	Hurricane IIc	S/Ldr C. P. N. Newman DFC
No.42 Sqn	Kangla	Hurricane IIc	S/Ldr G May DFC
No.60 Sqn	Agartala	Hurricane IIc	S/Ldr R. C. Lindsell RCAF
No.81 Sqn	Khumbirgram	Spitfire VIII	S/Ldr W. M. Whitamore DFC
			S/Ldr J. V. Marshall DFC
No.113 Sqn	Jorhat	Hurricane IIc	S/Ldr R. N. H. Courtney DFC
No.123 Sqn	Patharkandi	Hurricane IIc	S/Ldr A. J. McGregor

No.136 Sqn	Wangjing	Spitfire VIII	S/Ldr E. O. Watson
No.152 Sqn	Palel	Spitfire VIII	S/Ldr M. R. B. Ingram DFC
No.607 Sqn	Imphal	Spitfire VIII	S/Ldr G. G. A. Davies DFC
No.615 Sqn	Palel	Spitfire VIII	S/Ldr D. W. McCormack DFC
No.1 Sqn IAF	Imphal	Hurricane IIc	S/Ldr A. Singh DFC
No.9 Sqn IAF	Sikhar	Hurricane IIc	S/Ldr K. A. Perkin

Several of these squadrons sent detachments into the Imphal Valley during this period.

Major General Orde Charles Wingate DSO** was killed in a plane crash on 24 March 1944. He was forty-one years of age, had joined the Army in 1921 and saw service with the Royal Artillery, but found his forte organising special forces in Palestine in the 1930s and later in the Sudan and Abysinnia, for which he received the DSO in 1938 and a Bar in 1941. The second Bar to his DSO came in 1943; he was also awarded the *Lawrence of Arabia Memorial Medal* by the Royal Central Asian Society in 1943.

Operation THURSDAY was still underway when Wingate needed to fly to a conference. The RAF refused to do so because of very bad weather but an American B-25 pilot agreed to take him. The plane crashed in the bad conditions and the ten or so bodies found at the site were so badly burned that they could not be individually identified. They were buried near the crash site and later reinterred at Imphal. Later still the bodies were re-interred at Arlington National Cemetery in Virginia, USA, Wingate having to be placed with the rest because they could still not be separated through personal identification.

Palel airfield in the Imphal Valley. Hills rise to the right, the valley floor extends to the left. Everything withdrew into a central defensive position at night. Any buildings were open to light artillery fire as the Japanese held parts of the high ground.

Another view of Palel from the valley with hills surrounding its perimeter. The runway was little more than a dirt strip.

A Spitfire landing at Imphal. Rain had made large wet areas that needed to be avoided if a safe landing was to be made.

A regular sight on Burma airfields, and here on a wet Wangjing, the easiest way to move an aircraft was by muscle power. Although a couple of men wear capes, all the other airmen are in tropical dress – shorts, boots and bush hats.

The Wangjing 'Box'. Trenches, holes in the ground, sandbags, with poles, tarpaulins, and corrugated iron sheets for cover was how pilots and ground crews lived during the siege of Imphal. This was 607 Squadron's living area.

Squadron Leader G. G. A. Davies, CO of 607 Squadron, posing by his quarters, wearing his Mae West, although the nearest water mass is some distance away.

Airmen of 136 Squadron relaxing in their quarters at Wangjing during the siege.

Spitfire VIIIs of 81 Squadron,
Imphal Valley, 1944.

Spitfires of 607 Squadron at Imphal. Note the USAAF B-25 Mitchell on the runway. The nearest machine, GA-F, was the mount of Squadron Leader Graham Davies, 607's CO (JF890). Aircraft V was JG379.

Squadron Leader Graham Davies, CO 607 Squadron. He had fought over Dunkirk in 1940, and survived being brought down on the beach, then succeeded in getting himself on a ship back to England. He was wounded in the Battle of Britain with 222 Squadron, and survived more than forty fighter sweeps over France in 1941. Spitfire T was JG327.

Spitfire VIII of 615 Squadron at 'Readiness', Palel.

Hurricane IIs taxiing out at Palel to attack Japanese supply lines to the east and to the south.

Spitfire VIII, 607 Squadron at Imphal Main. Note the white identification patch on the tail fin. The machine in the foreground, AF-A (JF755), was usually flown by Flight Lieutenant Logan Briggs.

The airfield at Sapam, in the Imphal Valley, with Palel in the far distance.

The Palel airstrip, Imphal Valley. The circular spot to the left is where the aircraft were placed at night for protection against marauding Japanese soldiers.

Pilots of 136 Squadron (l to r): Dudley Barnett RAAF, Frank Wilding, Noel Constantine (CO), Gordon Conway and Denis Garvan RAAF. Wilding, Conway and Garvan were awarded DFCs for their actions over Burma.

Squadron Leader C. P. N. Newman DFC*, CO of 34 Squadron flying Hurricane fighter-bombers. His squadron operated close-support missions for the army in and around Kohima as well as attacking Japanese supply lines heading for Imphal.

Squadron Leader 'Ace' Newman's 34 Squadron Hurricane, LB792.

Close-up of 'Ace' Newman's Hurricane with one of his mechanics. Note the squadron leader's pennant on the cowling, with a frog with the inscription 'Baloney !!' The four 20mm cannon are for softening up the target area and keeping the enemy gunners' heads down during the run-in.

Squadron Leader J. A. Busbridge, CO of 34 (Fighter-bomber) Squadron. He had previously been a flight commander with 60 Squadron.

Hurricane of 9 Squadron Indian Air Force. Note the three elephants carrying supplies.

Squadron Leader K. A. Perkin seated in his 9 Squadron IAF Hurri-bomber. The tube-like feature stuck into the underside of the engine cowling is the attachment to the electric starter accumulator (trolly-acc).

More open air servicing, but at least the ground crew have Wellington boots. Note the accumulated junk strewn about and the box lid in the foreground that confirms this was 9 Squadron IAF at work.

Flight Sergeant I. D. Culpan RNZAF (right), 34 Squadron, with one of his ground crew on Palel airstrip. The insignia on the cowling shows the head of a lion with the words 'Jungle King' beneath it. Ian Culpan received the DFM in the summer of 1944.

Flight Sergeant Denny, 42 Squadron with his ground crew, Jenkins and Greensett. He flew 114 ops in this Hurricane, LB710 Q.

A 34 Squadron Hurricane taxiing out for a mission from Palel in 1944. Note the two bombs under the wings, the 20mm cannon, and a trolly-acc by the runway.

CHAPTER EIGHT

Air Battles over Imphal and the 'Late Arrivals Club'

With their soldiers being held up by the gallant defenders at Kohima, where the two sides were often no further apart than the width of the hill station's tennis court, the Japanese Army Air Force was really having a go at trying to suppress the RAF squadrons in the Imphal Valley. Oscars would scream in at zero feet trying to catch the RAF fighters on the ground, or would escort bombers in quick hit-and-run sorties against the airstrips. For their part the RAF fighter pilots would scramble into the air, often with the minimum of warning, and beat off these intrusions. In between times they would provide escort for the RAF and USAAF C-47s that were dropping desperately needed supplies to the Kohima defenders.

On 15 April 1944, 81 Squadron shot down one Oscar (Flying Officer D. W. Rathwell) and damaged two others during an early morning attack, while on the 17th they claimed another (by Alan Peart), damaged three more (two to Peart and one to Lieutenant J. G. White SAAF) and also knocked pieces off a Sally (White also). On the 25th, 81's pilots were once more in combat, with one Oscar destroyed (Don Rathwell again), one probable and six damaged (three to 'Bats' Krohn, one to White and one to Flight Sergeant B. E. Young RNZAF). The Oscar fighter was so nimble and the fighting often at low level, that it was dangerous to try and finish off any of these fighters that appeared to be going down, and so it was a case of just hitting them and breaking away. On the 26th, 615 Squadron claimed two probably destroyed, plus three damaged, while 607 Squadron got a probable and three damaged, and also damaged a Sally. This same day 81 Squadron knocked down a Dinah reconnaissance aircraft that disintegrated and fell in flames over Silchar, following the attention of Flight Lieutenant Bob Day and Lieutenant G. H. 'Shorty' Copeland SAAF. The Spitfire pilots now had the measure of intercepting these high-flying and fast recce machines.

No.607 probably shot down another on the 28th; Pilot Officer G. A. N. Curnock only claimed a probable, but in fact the Dinah failed to get home.

Another loss to the RAF occurred on 21 April 1944. Flying Officer James Gillies was serving with 136 Squadron, and had already had an interesting career. Jim Gillies was twenty-nine years old and had been a foster son to a family in Intake, Yorkshire. He had joined the RAF in 1935 as an aircraft-hand and later requested pilot training. Once trained, he was posted to 602 Squadron in September 1940 as a flight sergeant.

He saw action in the final weeks of the Battle of Britain and in October went to No. 421 Flight, which became 91 Squadron in 1941. He gained several victories and his gallant action culminated during the famous Channel Dash by German capital ships through the English Channel on 12 February 1942. This brought him the DFM in May and he was subsequently commissioned.

Joining 615 Squadron he moved with it to India and later joined 136 Squadron, with whom he shot down two Japanese aircraft in May 1943. He then became a flight commander with 79 Squadron. In March 1944 he seems to have been one of the RAF liaison officers with the Chindits. Going along with some ground forces, they penetrated to find a Japanese ammunition dump at Indaw. Returning, he explained the layout to the RAF and then, on 4 April, flying in a light communication aircraft, he flew to the spot and dropped smoke bombs from a mere fifty feet, whereupon RAF fighter-bombers blasted the dump with great accuracy. Sadly, back on operations on 21 April, he was shot down by ground fire and killed. The army had recommended him for the Military Cross for his actions on the 4th, and this was duly awarded – posthumously, the recommendation having been dated before his demise. He had accounted for six German and Japanese aircraft plus others damaged.

The month of May saw even more intense air fighting over the valley. No.607 Squadron had a string of successes in the first two weeks, with seven Oscars claimed destroyed plus eleven more damaged. Flying Officer Wilf Goold RAAF, got two of the confirmed victories. In the second half of May the pressure lessened but 615 Squadron still damaged a number of Oscars in the final days. All these victories came with surprisingly low casualties; 607 Squadron lost a pilot in combat on 18 May and 615 lost a pilot on the 29th, but that, apart from a number of Spitfires landing with various degrees of battle damage, was about all.

* *

Of course, the fighter-bomber Hurricanes suffered some casualties during their ground attack sorties, and some pilots were lost to bad weather. No.28 Squadron lost one on 7 April, 123 lost another on the 12th. On 25 April, Squadron Leader R. Lane suffered engine trouble and came down in the jungle. Roy Lane, a Battle of Britain pilot, was a pre-war airman who flew with 43 Squadron in 1940, and suffered burns when he was shot down. In 1942 he volunteered for MSFU (Merchant Ship Fighter Unit), going to sea with convoys, a Hurricane fitted to a merchant vessel in order for a pilot to be fired off if intercepted by long-range German bombers. More recently he had been with HQ ACSEA (Air Command, South-East Asia) and had volunteered to fly in to help the Chindits. He came down near the Chindwin river and was later seen on the ground. He was captured by the Japanese and beheaded sometime around 20 June. The Lane family lost three sons in the Second World War, two with the RAF and one with the Fleet Air Arm.

* *

There were other pilots, however, who survived being brought down in the Burmese jungle. One of the early accounts was for 7 December 1942, (the first anniversary of Pearl Harbor). No.607 had been in a scrap with enemy fighters and had lost two pilots, one being killed. However, the other, Sergeant R. W. Bates RCAF, became separated and then flew east instead of west to get home, ending up crash-landing in China. He then had to walk for several days, with just some rice to eat, to cover the 120-mile trek back home.

Another event, on 28 February 1943, concerned Sergeant D. J. Barnett RAAF, of 136 Squadron, who was shot down in his Hurricane by Captain Y. Kuroe of the 64th Sentai over Akyab Island, although he thought he had been hit by AA fire. Going down in flames he managed to bale out and landed in the sea, right in the mouth of the Mayu river. Despite enemy fighters still buzzing about he used his bright yellow dinghy and got ashore. The next day some natives took him a short way in a canoe but then he had a two-mile swim across the Mayu with its attendant crocodiles. With his desert boots sucked off in deep mud he had to continue barefooted without food or water. Eventually he was helped by more natives who took him to a British outpost. It had taken Dudley Barnett four days to reach safety, having gained membership of the 'Caterpillar Club', 'The Goldfish Club' and the 'Late Arrivals Club' all in one go. He was later commissioned and survived the war.

On 22 March 1944, 113 Squadron's Hurri-bombers were out and three became separated from the main formation in rain and low cloud. Flying Officers J. A. Illman RCAF, A. L. Herbert and Sergeant H. Clement soon ran short of fuel and, seeing an airstrip, quickly landed. Unfortunately it was Tamu, now occupied by the Japanese, although none were in immediate attendance. Leaving Clement to stay by the aircraft, the two officers went off to find someone, but soon he heard shots and assuming they came from the enemy, he quickly dived into a nearby monsoon drain, shortly before Japanese soldiers turned up. Seeing three aircraft they began to search for the missing pilot but Clement remained concealed. Even when some Hurricanes arrived and proceeded to strafe the three aircraft on the ground he kept himself hidden.

As the turmoil ended, 'Curly' Clement quickly slipped into the jungle and spent the next two weeks making his way through the jungle, clambering up and down hills and valleys, whilst Japanese soldiers continued their search for him. He finally made his way into the Imphal Valley and walked into Palel on 7 April. John Illman and Aubrey Herbert were never seen again and their deaths were assumed on their day of loss, shot by the Japanese.

Also on 22 March, 34 Squadron had a pilot fail to return, this being Flying Officer R. E. Jackson. However, he managed to bale out, successfully evaded the Japanese and walked back to Allied lines.

Flying Officer D. H. Hamblyn RNZAF, of 81 Squadron, was shot down by an Oscar on 18 May 1944 and crash-landed near Moirang. He, too, managed to evade capture and started to walk back. Fortunately for him he was found and picked up by an army patrol and brought back to base.

On 5 June 1944, Warrant Officer J. M. Bott of 113 Squadron, was shot down by ground fire north-east of Imphal. John Bott was on his thirty-fourth mission. His was the fifth Hurricane to make its approach to the target, but was not happy with his run-in, and decided to go round again. As he did so he felt a thud and, pulling up, his engine quit. Still only 200 feet or so in the air, he was quickly bellying in, climbing out and running for cover. The rest of the squadron were circling round and seeing him run clear, dived down and shot-up the pranged fighter.

Bott began crawling away, reached a bend in the Iril river and took cover till sunset, before setting off westwards. Keeping direction by compass, he scrambled up and down numerous hills. His only sustenance (apart from a few Horlicks tablets) was from sucking dew off leaves and grass. Later he found some water by digging in a dry nullah (a small stream or ditch), then headed on through bamboo canes and elephant grass, with all manner of flying insects buzzing round his head. He eventually got back, finally running into two Sikh soldiers who brought him to safety. Bott found that a recce Hurricane had photographed his burning fighter on the ground and gave him a copy.

There were other fighter pilots who failed to return from missions, but whether they were killed immediately or died trying to walk out of the deadly jungle terrain – or taken and killed by the Japanese – will never be known. Flying Officer Ray Crossfield RCAF from Ontario, aged twenty-two, of 136 Squadron was just one. On 13 April 1944 he simply disappeared returning from an escort to supply-dropping aircraft to a Chindit airstrip. Soldiers later found the Spitfire and it seemed the pilot had survived the crash landing but not the walk back.

For one six-month period between September 1944 and March 1945, there is a figure of 176 aircrew being forced down over the Burmese jungles, of whom 166 were never seen again. Of the ten who did walk out, only three made it back from Japanese-held territory.

* *

The Burmese weather was yet another danger for RAF pilots. On 15 June 1944, 615 Squadron had three of their pilots killed in a storm. The Squadron had been escorting supply drop aircraft helping the Chindits around Indawggyi Lake and Myitkyina. As they returned, they encountered huge cloud formations that reached up to some 40,000 feet. Once out of the Imphal Valley, as these Spitfires were on this operation, the high mountainous terrain impeded the limited scope of the few D/F stations that existed. It was a three-and-three-quarter-hour flight, with drop tanks but, once they hit this weather front, everyone lost touch and, without sight of the ground, each pilot had to fly by his own dead reckoning to get back. Three failed to do so, Pilot Officer Bill Hyde and Flight Sergeants E. Kennedy and J. McKay were never seen again. No.615 Squadron would suffer a similar tragedy in August.

Two days later, on the 17th, 615 and 607 Squadrons, including Wing Commander P. H. Lee (OC 170 Wing), got into an air fight with some Oscars in the late morning, Kevin Gannon and Chat Chatfield of 615 each claiming one, Flying Officer C. F. Bush probably destroying another. Pat Lee claimed two while 607 netted two, one by Squadron Leader Davies, one and a damaged by Flying Officer H. Taylor. The Japanese had not been over the valley for more than a week and had not been engaged by Spitfires since 29 May.

The actions on the 17th began with 615 Squadron putting up a section which found some Japanese transport on the Tiddim road which they strafed; they then shot up two sampans they spotted on the Chindwin. Pat Lee had been on an air test when things began to happen, radar picking up approaching hostiles. Spitfires of 607 scrambled and 615 Squadron also put up another section. Group HQ in Imphal had received a call from an observation post, reporting an estimated twenty Japanese aircraft, heading north at 8,000 feet. No.81 Squadron then also put up a section of Spitfires. Tactics had recently been improved so that when Japanese aircraft were reported, Spitfires would get airborne and head for pre-arranged positions near to where gaps in the mountains usually found enemy aircraft flying through rather than risking climbing over them.

By this time, with all the activity farther north and east, the Japanese strength had been somewhat depleted, and one Japanese squadron had been withdrawn to Sumatra. Now, however, the Japanese sent fourteen Oscars to Imphal and, when these met RAF fighters, a mighty battle ensued, with the results mentioned above. In all, the Spitfire pilots claimed six destroyed, four probables and one damaged. In fact the Japanese lost five in total, and claimed two Spitfires, although only one was lost. This was Warrant Officer J. E. Payne RAAF, of 615 Squadron, who later walked back. He and his twin brother, Pilot Officer A. A. Payne, both flew with 615 Squadron, a fairly rare occurrence. They were Australians.

By July the approach of the monsoon began to curtail operations once again, but in any event the Japanese attempts to take the valley and overcome the Kohima garrison had failed and they began to withdraw. Soon after a relief force broke through to Kohima. The Japanese would never return and their full retreat began in earnest, especially with the taking of Meiktila by the Chindits and General Stilwell's forces.

Written on a memorial that was later erected at Kohima, are some poignant words that are often read during Remembrance Services every 11 November, although not just referring to Kohima:

When you go home, tell them of us and say,
For their tomorrow, we gave our today.

* *

Japanese domination in Burma very quickly slipped away. Some Japanese tanks had made an attempt to enter the valley along the Tiddim road, but got no more than twenty miles before Hurricanes bombed and strafed them. By now Spitfires, too, were being used for ground strafing Japanese troops and mechanical transport, although this was not favoured by HQ as they were deemed too important flying air cover to protect fighter-bombers and transport aircraft. Both sieges, Imphal and Kohima, were finally over and the Japanese were on the run.

Two stalwarts of 607 Squadron. Warrant Officer K. F. Longley and Flying Officer R. W. Bates RCAF. Longley had been wounded in combat on 5 March 1943 but got back to operations and featured in dogfights in early 1944. It was Bobby Bates who, in December 1942, had become separated from the squadron, flew east rather than west, and ended up in China. It took him several days to walk back.

Dudley Barnett RAAF, 136 Squadron. Shot down over Akyab Island on 28 February 1943, he survived a bale out into the Mayu estuary, and later a two-mile swim across the river. Evading through the jungle, he was eventually found by British troops after four days.

Curly Clement and Joe Ward of 113 Squadron. Clement was lucky to escape execution on 22 March 1944 after he and two companions lost their way and landed on Tamu airstrip in error. The others were killed by Japanese troops but Clement managed to trek back through jungle and steep hills to reach Imphal more than two weeks later.

Flying Officer D. H. Hamblyn of 81 Squadron. Shot down in combat on 18 May 1944, he evaded capture and walked back through dense jungle before being found by British soldiers. The garlands and flowers celebrate his safe return.

John Bott of 113 Squadron was forced to crash-land his Hurricane on 5 June 1944, following a hit by ground fire. He evaded Japanese patrols looking for him. Eventually he ran into two Sikh soldiers after three days and they brought him to safety.

John Bott's downed Hurricane was strafed by RAF fighters and set on fire while he was hiding in nearby undergrowth about to start his three-day trek to safety. He was lucky to be over fairly open country, for a crash-landing in jungle was not usually successful.

As the Imphal siege reached its conclusion, the Japanese made repeated fighter sweeps over the valley and were met by determined RAF fighter pilots ready to join combat. Flying Officer Wilf Goold RAAF gained several victories at this time and received the DFC in June. He had been in theatre for two years.

Flight Lieutenant I. R. 'Bats' Krohn had flown in North Africa before being posted to Burma in early 1944. He also had successes over Imphal in 1944 with 81 Squadron and subsequently commanded 155 Squadron. His DFC was announced later that year. On the right is Wing Commander P. H. Lee, a pre-war pilot who had been an instructor for the first years of the war. After flying night-fighters and then Typhoons, he was posted to India and took command of 170 Wing. He gained several combat successes and was awarded the DFC.

Warrant Officer Bill Townend, 607 Squadron, in the untold luxury of the Wangjng Box. On 28 April 1944 he and Pilot Officer G. A. N. Curnock made persistent attacks on a recce Dinah near Imphal which, when it disappeared off the RAF's radar, was thought to be destroyed but could only be claimed as a 'probable'. In the event, however, the Japanese aircraft, from the 81st Sentai, failed to reach home.

Two Burmese pilots flew with 607 Squadron, Flying Officers S. S. Shi-Sho and L. S. Main. Sadly, Main was killed in action on 15 March 1943, but Sammy Shi-Sho continued to fly combat and was involved in the air fighting over the Imphal Valley in 1944. Shi-Sho later rose to command the Burmese Air Force. Lam Shai Main was a Sino Burmese, Shi-Sho a Karen.

Three of the top men in Burma, Air Marshal Stanley Vincent DFC AFC, AOC No.221 Group RAF, General Sir William 'Bill' Slim CBE DSO MC, commander Fourteenth Army, and Air Marshal Sir Alex Coryton CB MVO DFC, Air Officer Commanding 3rd Tactical Air Force (3TAF).

No.615 Squadron on the move along the road through Kohima after the battle. Burma was always difficult terrain to traverse.

Admiral Lord Louis Mountbatten, Supreme Commander SEAC (South-East Asia Command), decorating Squadron Leader A. Singh with the DFC, May 1944. Arjan Singh commanded No.1 Squadron Indian Air Force (Hurricanes). Standing behind Mountbatten is Air Marshal S. F. Vincent DFC AFC, and far right is Air Marshal Sir John Baldwin KBE CB DSO, Air Officer Commanding 3rd Tactical Air Force.

Pilots of No.34 Squadron, flying Hurri-bombers. In the centre, front row, is Flight Lieutenant J. H. Whalen DFC RCAF; others identified standing (l to r): Flying Officer Lyndon-Moore, Taffy David, Flight Sergeant Day, Sergeant Beales, Flight Lieutenant Ricky Richmond, Vic Sole, ?,?. Seated: -?-, Sergeant Kirby, Flight Sergeant Hodsman, ?, Whalen, Hank Weston, Les Cowan, Flight Sergeant Stevens. Jimmy Whalen, from Vancouver, was an extremely experienced fighter pilot, having flown in the Western Desert after a tourwith Fighter Command over France in 1941. Moving to the Far East he saw action over Ceylon in April 1942 with 30 Squadron and then, following a periodof instructing, joined 34 Squadron. After numerous ground attack sorties, his squadron was ordered to knock out a particularly obstinate Japanese bunker on 18 April 1944. They failed, but Jimmy requested that he go in again. This time he was hit by ground fire, crashed and was killed. His DFC was announced in 1945, but back-dated prior to his death.

Flying Officer J. N. Yates DFC, 607 Squadron. 'Banger' Yates was another Burma 'ace', his victories scored between late 1942 and early 1944, in both Hurricanes and Spitfires.

Flying Officer James Gillies MC DFM. Gillies had served at the tail-end of the Battle of Britain and, operating during 1941 and early 1942, had received the DFM. Posted to the Far East he had flown with 136 Squadron and later became a flight commander with 79 Squadron. Attached to the Chindits in March 1944 he had been on a ground patrol with the army and, near Indaw, found a Japanese ammunition dump. Returning to report this, he flew out in a light aircraft on 4 April and marked the target with smoke bombs from fifty feet, whereupon the dump was smashed by RAF aircraft. The army recommended the MC for this feat, but sadly, he was killed in action on 21 April, shot down by ground fire. On the right is Flight Lieutenant John. S. Hart who had served in the Battle of Britain, and in 1941, with 91 Squadron as Gillies's flight commander. Posted to the Far East, he flew with 9 Squadron IAF, then commanded 67 Squadron in 1943.

CHAPTER NINE
Finalé

The RAF continued to support Fourteenth Army as they chased the Japanese out of Burma. Fighter combat became rare, but there were ample opportunities to attack the enemy on the ground. As had been expected, the Allies had prevailed during the ground battles due, to a large extent, to the RAF's supply-dropping missions, while the Japanese had suffered greatly due to lack of food and water, as well as armaments with which to fight.

Life on the airstrips in the Imphal Valley had been tough but everyone had pulled together and had overcome the siege. Some of the conditions in which the air and ground crews lived, worked and fought were not always thought to be appreciated by the 'brass' in way-off Delhi, and their occasional visits to the various 'boxes' in the valley were not universally welcomed by the rank and file. No. 34 Squadron at Palel, had a Doctor Paddy Fee, who had abhorred the sanitary conditions in particular, in which he had to work, so when a high-ranking medical officer from Delhi arrived and began commenting, Paddy wrote the following ditty, which everyone appreciated.

(In truth it covered almost anywhere in Burma.)

Bullshit and brass from Delhi afar,
Stepped haughtily down from his bloody great car,
Into a cesspool filled up with shit,
Enquired for Palel,
And was told, this is it!

By the end of May 1944 the monsoon weather was becoming steadily worse. On the last day of May two Hurricane pilots were lost, due to a great extent by the weather. One was from 42 Squadron, the other from 20 Squadron. Lord Mountbatten continued to implement the doctrine that operations should not be stopped by monsoon conditions but, of course, the scale of operations was again much reduced. Several RAF squadrons took the opportunity for a break, and were sent back to India or at least to airfields away from the front.

July saw the monsoon at full force, but whenever possible the RAF dropped supplies to the troops on the ground. Hurricanes continued to suffer losses, 34 losing one on the 7th and 60 Squadron another on the 8th. No.42 Squadron lost yet another on the 20th. The key base at Myitkyina, almost on the Chinese border, by the Irrawaddy in the north, was finally relieved on 3 August. Continuing south down this river lay Mandalay in central Burma. The mighty Irrawaddy, of course, headed straight down to Magwe and, finally, Rangoon, the ultimate prize.

RAF aircraft increased their attacks upon Japanese vessels along the Chindwin, but care had to be taken, as the enemy often strung wires across it in an attempt to bring down low-flying Hurricanes or twin-engined Beaufighters. As August began 60 Squadron lost another Hurricane and pilot and 211 Squadron a Beau with its crew. However, the worst day in terms of loss due to weather came on 10 August 1944.

The pilots of 615 Squadron were ordered to fly from Dergaon to Bagachi, east of Calcutta. They were well due for a rest. Led by Squadron Leader D. W. McCormack DFC*, the weather was fine at base but approaching Calcutta they found a huge thunderhead in their path. There was no way around it and it quickly enveloped the sixteen Spitfires in its thick dark brown monsoon storm. Unfortunately, the pilots had reached a point where low levels in fuel tanks did not permit the option of a return to Dergaon. It was Calcutta or nothing. McCormack tried to lead his men up, round and over the storm but suddenly the cloud became very thick and very black, and full of hailstones and swirling winds.

One Spitfire crashed into McCormack's machine while others were being tossed about, mostly out of sight of each other. Four pilots were killed, another crash-landed, suffering just minor injuries, while three more baled out, all receiving leg injuries; eight Spitfires in total were lost.

Operations against retreating Japanese forces continued when possible but it was still a dangerous business. On 18 August, for instance, Hurricanes of 11 Squadron and Spitfires of 152 Squadron were strafing and lost one Hurricane whose pilot crashed into a river; another loss was due to ground fire, this machine crashing in flames by the Tiddim Road. No.152 Squadron had a pilot hit a tree and crash to his death.

* *

For almost a year now the RAF had been sending their new and their experienced fighter pilots through a unique unit based at Amarda Road, Orissa, India. Its commanding officer and chief instructor was Wing Commander Frank Carey DFC** DFM. Carey, it will be remembered, fought over Rangoon and Burma in late 1941 and into 1942, during the retreat towards Chittagong. Nobody who had flown with him had any doubt that his ability as a fighter pilot was way above exceptional, so there was no better person to instruct and instil in Burma fighter pilots just how to combat the enemy's fighter pilots. For this work he would receive the Air Force Cross, while the Americans would award him their Silver Star, for US pilots too had received his words of wisdom on courses.

He was able to virtually hand-pick his instructors from the men he knew and respected from the fighter squadrons in Burma, several of whom were being rested. As mentioned earlier, fighter pilots in Burma rarely returned to Britain after an elongated tour of operations, and most were proud to be associated with Frank and his air fighting school.

Frank had initially set this up in February 1943 and in June had flown back to the UK to attend a Central Gunnery Course at RAF Sutton Bridge, Norfolk. He returned in September and began instructing his instructors who in turn took courses of pilots to either prepare them for combat or hone their skills for further action.

Among his select band of instructors were: Robin Hedderwich DFC (607), W. D. 'Jimmy' James (607), Eric Batchelar (17), Paul Lousi DFC DFM (615), 'Banger' Yates DFC (607), A. F. C. 'Val' Valentine (615), Brian Verry (615), Jack Storey (135), and Guy Marsland (136). Once established, whole squadrons would be sent to Amarda Road, receive Carey's words of wisdom and then return to the front.

* *

September 1944 saw a slight improvement in the weather, but on the 3rd, 155 Squadron, which had replaced the unfortunate 615 Squadron in mid-August, commenced operations. It was based at Palel with Spitfire VIIIs and the CO was Squadron Leader Ian Krohn. In May 1945, Squadron Leader Gordon Conway DFC, late of 136 Squadron, would take over from Krohn till the war's end. On 7 October 1944, Flight Lieutenant T. Hunter of 155, shot down a Dinah in flames from 29,000 feet south-east of Tamu.

During September the RAF began to receive a new fighter aeroplane. New to the RAF, but not new to the war, the American Republic P-47 Thunderbolt had been used by the USAAF in Europe since the US 8th Air Force came to Britain, and despite its size and weight, was a very capable fighter in the hands of its pilots. The Hurricane was now getting old, and the Thunderbolt was seen as its natural replacement. No.5 Squadron was the first RAF unit so equipped in Burma to be used as fighter-bombers and flew 'cab-rank' sorties, directed to targets by visual control personnel behind the front line, who could call them up and direct their attacks, often by having the artillery firing coloured smoke where they should drop their bombs. They carried eight .50-inch calibre guns and three bombs, one under each wing and one beneath the fuselage, to a total weight of 2,000 lbs. Their heavy armament wreaked havoc among the Japanese troops, motor transport and strongpoints. In October, 134 and 258 Squadrons began to receive P-47s, known in the RAF as Thunderbolt Is. No.79 Squadron, too, would soon head into Wangjing with Thunderbolts, under command of Squadron Leader Ken Hemingway, who had been with 17 Squadron in the early Burma days.

While the Dakota supply aircraft were flying in constant danger from ground fire, they were not often attacked by enemy fighters, but on 8 November such an attack occurred. Dropping supplies to ground forces at Kalemyo, some seventy miles south of the Imphal Valley, Oscars engaged them, shooting down three RAF machines and three Americans. No.152 Squadron scrambled Spitfires but arrived too late. On the 11th, Warrant Officer E. R. Griffiths of 146 Squadron, who had been in action over Calcutta in December 1943, and was now flying Thunderbolts, was hit by ground fire whilst attacking Meiktila and became a prisoner of war, ending up in Rangoon jail.

Thunderbolts were generally used for ground attack sorties but on 17 November 135 Squadron got into a fight with some Ki-43s and Pilot Officer R. E. Windle with Flight Sergeant Maxwell, claimed the RAF Thunderbolt's first victory. The squadron damaged two others. Another first for the Thunderbolt came on 1 December, with this aircraft using napalm for the first time against ground targets. No.258 Squadron, using a mixture of Thunderbolt Is and the improved Mark IIs, dive-bombed Magwe on the 7th, an airfield the RAF had so unceremoniously been kicked out of back in 1942.

During an attack on bridges at Kaing on 27 November, 60 Squadron lost a Hurricane and 1 IAF Squadron also lost one flying a Tac/R mission, its pilot deciding to strafe some bashas. Flying Officer D. F. Eduljee, aged twenty-three, the first Indian Air Force recipient of an Air Force Cross, was shot down and killed. Since its arrival into Imphal in February 1944, this squadron had lost nine of its pilots.

At the start of the new year of 1945, the following fighter squadrons were under control of 221 Group:

No.1 IAF Sqn	Imphal	Hurricane IIc	S/Ldr R Ranjaram DFC
No.607 Sqn	Tulihal	Spitfire VIII	S/Ldr G. G. A. Davies DFC
No.79 Sqn	Wangjing	Thunderbolt	S/Ldr R. D. May
No.146 Sqn	Wangjing	Thunderbolt	S/Ldr R. A. C. Weir
No.261 Sqn	Wangjing	Thunderbolt	S/Ldr P. C. Fletcher DFC
No.11 Sqn	Tamu	Hurricane IIc	S/Ldr G. A. Butler
No.28 Sqn	Tamu	Hurricane IIc	S/Ldr H. G. F. Larsen DFC
No.17 Sqn	Taukkyan	Spitfire VIII	S/Ldr J. H. Lacey DFM*
No.20 Sqn	Sapam	Hurricane IId	S/Ldr A. R. Miller DFC
No.155 Sqn	Sapam	Spitfire VIII	S/Ldr I. R. Krohn DFC
No.34 Sqn	Yazagyo	Hurricane IIc	S/|Ldr J. A. Busbridge
No.113 Sqn	Yazagyo	Hurricane IIc	S/Ldr J. Rose DFC
No.42 Sqn	Kangla	Hurricane IIc	S/Ldr J. G. Fogg FDC
No.60 Sqn	Kangla	Hurricane IIc	S/Ldr J. S. Humphreys

On the Arakan front the Allied forces were starting to push the Japanese back too. In the air 67 Squadron engaged some Ki-84 'Frank' fighters, on 9 January 1945, although the RAF had not yet identified this new fighter, and thought they were Oscars. Squadron Leader R. W. R. Day RCAF shot down two, Flight Lieutenant C. M. Simpson also claimed two, while Warrant Officer P. M. McQuarrie claimed another. The Franks had been attacking shipping off Akyab Island using 250kg bombs, and some accompanying Oscars carried 100kg bombs.

Akyab Island was retaken and then, on 21 January, Allied troops landed on Ramree Island. New airfields were quickly provided for fighters, fighter-bombers and transport aircraft. The net was beginning to tighten. Two pilots of 67 Squadron shot down a Dinah over Ramree on 10 February; Flight Lieutenant E. G. Hickey and Flight Sergeant J. L. Ellington had engaged the recce machine at 35,000 feet.

There were still some very experienced pilots in action in this the last year of the war. No.258 Squadron was commanded by Squadron Leader N. Cameron DFC, and he shared the destruction of a Ki-61 'Tony' fighter with the gunners of a 215 Squadron Liberator over Rangoon on 11 February. Two days later, Squadron Leader J. H. Lacey DFM*, shot down an Oscar south of Mandalay. 'Ginger' Lacey had seen action over France and during the Battle of Britain in 1940, and later on sweeps over France. Soon some units of the Japanese Army Air Force were being ordered not to engage large formations of Allied aircraft because of the high losses being sustained. They were fast running out of aeroplanes and, of course, experienced pilots.

Then Mandalay fell. Its defence had cost the Japanese over 12,000 casualties. Meiktila had also fallen, costing the enemy a further 6,500 casualties. The Japanese were now retreating towards Rangoon.

The Japanese 64th Sentai, a unit that had seen considerable action over Burma since the start, claimed its final victory in Burma on 24 April, a pilot of 17 Squadron, over Toungoo during an attack on British MT. They had their last combat action on the 29th, again with 17 Squadron's Spitfire VIIIs.

May 1945 saw the Allies starting to prepare to scale down operations in Burma, deciding upon 1 June, or at least, when Rangoon was recaptured, in order to concentrate on other areas in the region. On 2 May, while preparations to advance into the capital were underway, it was discovered that, in fact, the Japanese had gone. With the enemy now in full retreat, mostly on foot, or using river craft, and with virtually no air opposition left, Allied fighters were flying more and more cab rank sorties against any retreating troops they found. The Japanese tried to withdraw across the Sittang river in July, the RAF sending every available aircraft in to attack – over 3,000 sorties being recorded. This was virtually the last fighting on the Burma front, and in nine days it was estimated that some 10,000 enemy soldiers had been killed, bringing Japanese losses in Burma to around 100,000.

RAF fighter squadrons as at 30 June 1945, under 221 Group, now at Rangoon, were as follows:

No.906 Wing			
No.28 Sqn	Mingaladon	Hurricane IIc	S/Ldr J. Rhind
No.273 Sqn	Mingaladon	Spitfire VIII	S/Ldr L. A. Thorogood DFC
No.607 Sqn	Baigachi	Spitfire VIII	S/Ldr C. J. O. Pegge DFC
No.909 Wing			
No.152 Sqn	Thedaw	Spitfire VIII	S/Ldr G. Kerr DFC
No.155 Sqn	Toungoo	Spitfire VIII	S/Ldr A. G. Conway DFC
No.910 Wing			
No.34 Sqn	Kinmagan	Thunderbolt	S/Ldr G. T. A. Douglas DFC
No.113 Sqn	Kinmagan	Thunderbolt	S/Ldr M. Paddle
No.42 Sqn	Dulbumgarh	Hurricane IIC	S/Ldr J. G. Fogg DFC
No.79 Sqn	Meiktila	Thunderbolt	S/Ldr R. D. May

Other squadrons recently engaged in operations on the Burma front had now moved back for a rest. These RAF fighter units were:

No.222 Group, Colombo			
No.346 Wing			
No.136 Sqn	Cocos Islands	Spitfire VIII	S/Ldr A. J. H. Kitley
No.224 Group, Madras			
No.902 Wing			
No.11 Sqn	Chettinad	Spitfire XIV	S/Ldr B. T. Shannon
No.904 Wing			
No.134 Sqn	Kyaukpyu	Thunderbolt	S/Ldr C. G. Ford
No.258 Sqn	Ulunderpet	Thunderbolt	S/Ld N. Cameron DFC
No.905 Wing			
No.5 Sqn	Vizagapatam	Thunderbolt	S/Ldr L. H. Dawes DFC
No.30 Sqn	Chakulia	Thunderbolt	S/Ldr T. H. Meyer
No.615 Sqn	Chakulia	Thunderbolt	S/Ldr P. J. Anson DFC
No.123 Sqn	Bobbili	Thunderbolt	S/Ldr A. J. McGregor
No.81 Sqn	Bobbili	Thunderbolt	S/Ldr P. A. Kennedy DFC

No.907 Wing			
No.20 Sqn	St Thomas Mount	Hurricane IId	S/Ldr A. R. Miller DFC

The air war had finally come to an end, although in the north American fighter pilots were still engaging the last of the Japanese machines still operating. British and American air power had swamped the Japanese efforts and on the ground Allied troop numbers exceeded the Japanese by some three to one. Allied aircraft in theatre already numbered almost 1,000 at the time of Imphal and had reached 1,500 by the end of 1944.

General fighting ended on 20 August 1945 with the Japanese surrender. Some isolated resistance continued for some days, but the war with Japan was finally over and Burma had been retaken. While the land battle had been hard fought and hard won by British, Indian, Gurkha, American and Chinese soldiers, without the support of the RAF and the USAAF, plus elements of the Fleet Air Arm in the latter stages, the fight would have been far from decided. While the fighter pilots had kept the Japanese fighters at bay for most of the time, and fighter-bombers had aided the soldiers' advances, it had been the British and American air supply squadrons that had made the difference. Had they failed to support the Admin Box in the Arakan, or the defenders of Kohima in the north, India might well have had a very different tale to tell. These mostly unsung heroes are worthy of the utmost praise and approbation.

Very often history of the Burma campaign, when compiled by the army, gave little credit to the RAF's part, but Field Marshal Sir William Slim, in his book *Defeat into Victory* (published in 1956) noted his appreciation for the work by the RAF. He said, 'Rarely can so small an Air Force have battled so gallantly and so effectively against a comparable foe.'

Lord Louis Mountbatten visiting 9 Squadron IAF at Cox's Bazar 1944. 'Can you all see me?'

Pilots of 615 Squadron. (l to r): Flying Officer M. Paine RAAF, Warrant Officer A. A. Payne, Flying Officer Roy Laycock, Flying Officer M. S. Fulford RAAF, Flight Lieutenant G. Falconer, Squadron Leader D. W. McCormack DFC, Flight Lieutenant K. Gannon, Warrant Officer A. Chapple RAAF, Pilot Officer P. Whitman, Flight Sergeant H. B. Chatfield, Warrant Officer J. E. Payne. A. A. Payne and J. E. Payne were twins. On 10 August 1944, McCormack, M. Paine, and Chapple were killed when flying into a huge thunderstorm.

Pilot Officer W. S. Bond RCAF of 615 was another fatality due to the storm on 10 August 1944.

Officers of 152 Squadron at Tulihal, on 20 September 1944: (l to r) Eric Clegge, Geoff Duval, 'Dingha' Bell, Jimmy Chuck, Black, Vic Vickers, Bob Ainsworth, Bluey Human, Ron Partridge. The squadron was heavily involved in escorts, armed reconnaissance and ground attack sorties.

Spitfires of 152 Squadron in July 1945 while at Imphal. Note the white identification stripes on the wings and elevators, plus a white tail patch. Aircraft 'C' (MT982) survived until June 1946.

View of typical terrain in Burma. This is a British convoy on the Manipur Road after the siege of Imphal, but it demonstrates the danger of fighter aircraft strafing any convoy, Allied or Japanese, in such conditions.

Squadron Leader L. C. C. Hawkins DSO DFC, commanding officer of 135 Squadron seated on the wing of his Thunderbolt II. The fighter's 0.50 calibre guns are clear to see. Lee Hawkins commanded the unit from May 1944 until June 1945, the period it was flying Thunderbolts. He had been with 135 since the retreat from Rangoon in 1942, fought in the Arakan battles and then commanded it in the final stages of the Burma war. It was renumbered 615 Squadron in June 1945.

Republic Thunderbolts of 135 Squadron in December 1944. Aircraft A was HD173, while just beyond it is aircraft D HB982. It was in this aircraft that Bob Windle claimed the first Japanese aircraft shot down by an RAF Thunderbolt.

Bob Windle, 135 Squadron. Another long-serving pilot with this unit who had gradually risen in rank, he shot down the first Japanese aircraft to fall to an RAF Thunderbolt on 17 November 1944. This photgraph was taken in Calcutta, with Red Road in the background.

RAF Thunderbolt II NA-F (HD295) flown by 146 Squadron at Kumbhrigram in October 1944.

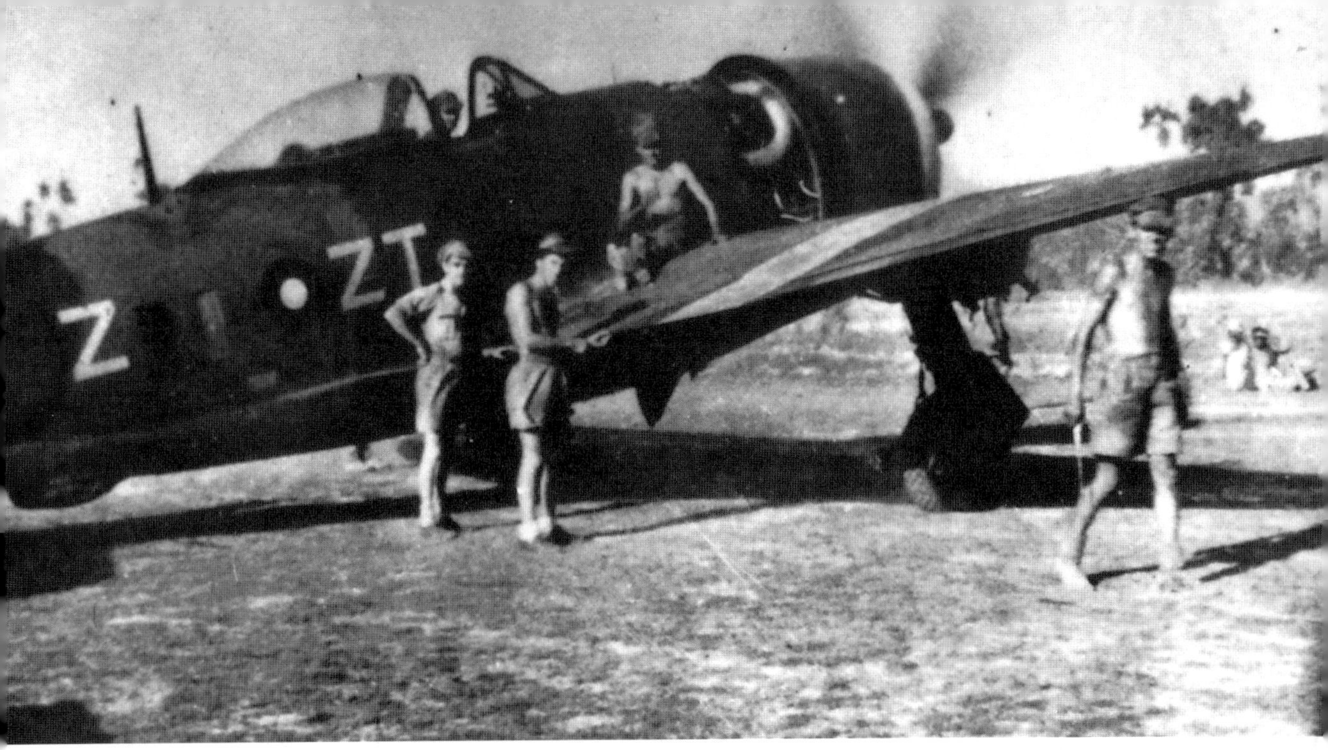

Thunderbolt II, HZ244 ZT-Z, of 258 Squadron, Ratnap, January 1945

Squadron Leader Neil Cameron DFC, OC 258 Squadron. He shared a Ki-61 fighter over Rangoon with an RAF Liberator on 11 February 1945.

Squadron Leader Bob Day DFC driving, with Flight Lieutenant C. M. Simpson in the passenger seat, both 67 Squadron. These two shot down Ki-84 fighters on 9 January 1945. The Spitfire has the name *Mary Ann* on its nose.

Pilots of 34 Squadron at Palel during a briefing on 1 December 1944. The Hurricane marked 'X' was LD261 which suffered an undercarriage collapse at Onbauk, north of Mandalay, on 9 March 1945.

Another long-serving fighter pilot was Squadron Leader D. K. McDonald DSO DFC from New South Wales, Australia. He had flown with 130, 30, 136 and 261 Squadrons before taking command of 134 Squadron in May 1944 and had flown Hurricanes, Spitfires and Thunderbolts. He was known as 'Aussie Mac'.

Flying Officer F. E. Wilding DFC of 136 Squadron. Frank saw action with the squadron between 1942 and 1944; like so many, a very long period of operational flying with the same unit. During this time he rose from sergeant to commissioned rank and accounted for four certain victories, two 'probables' and two damaged. The name *Barbara* on his Spitfire refers to the girl he met in India and married. She was the daughter of a local Kalamazoo agent, for whom Frank had worked in England pre-war.

Maps

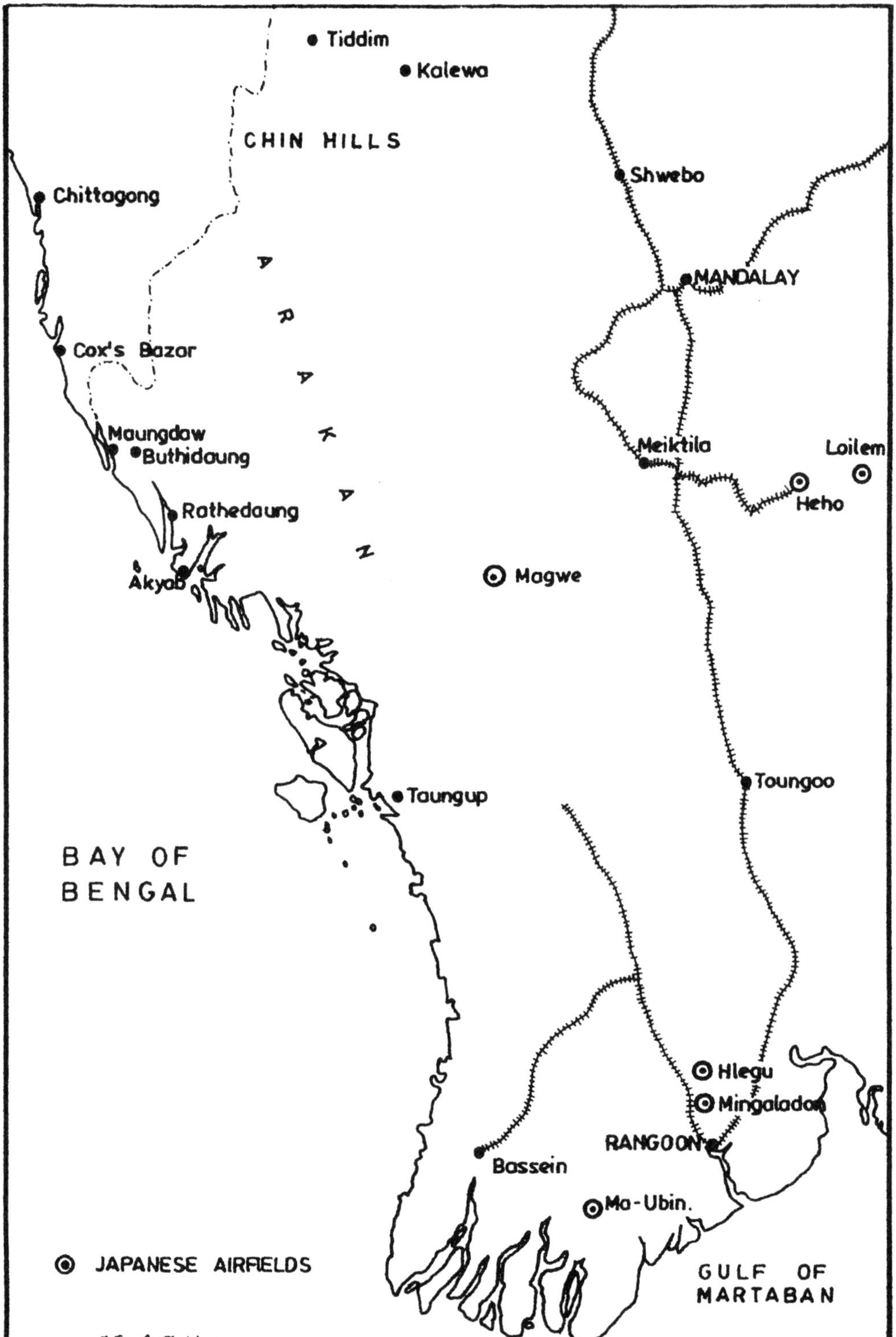
Tiddim
Kalewa
CHIN HILLS
Chittagong
Shwebo
MANDALAY
ARAKAN
Cox's Bazar
Maungdaw
Buthidaung
Rathedaung
Meiktila
Loilem
Heho
Akyab
Magwe
Taungup
Toungoo
BAY OF
BENGAL
Hlegu
Mingaladon
RANGOON
Bassein
Ma-Ubin.
JAPANESE AIRFIELDS
GULF OF
MARTABAN

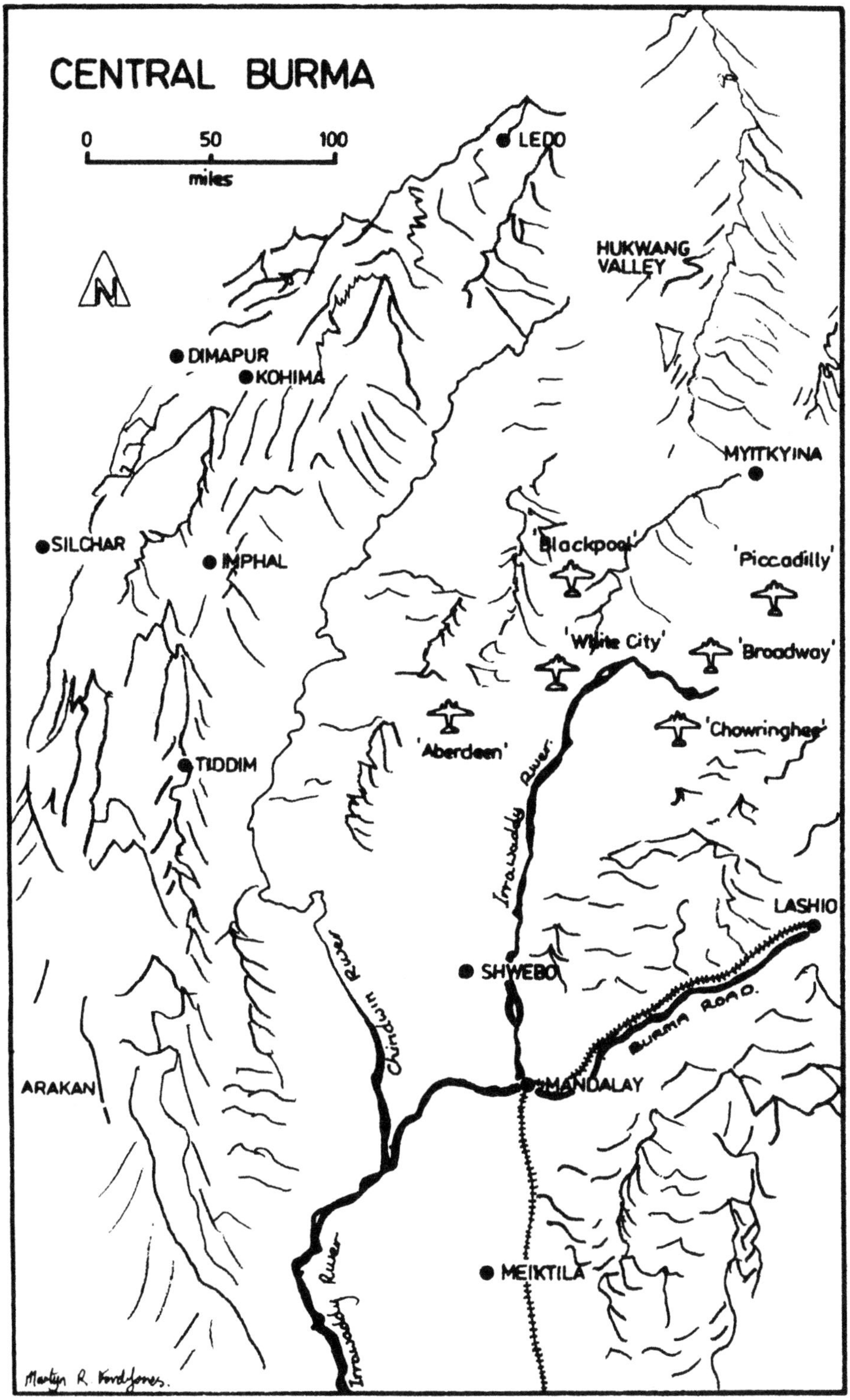
CENTRAL BURMA
0
50
100
miles
N
LEDO
HUKWANG VALLEY
DIMAPUR
KOHIMA
MYITKYINA
SILCHAR
IMPHAL
'Blackpool'
'Piccadilly'
'White City'
'Broadway'
'Aberdeen'
'Chowringhee'
TIDDIM
Irrawaddy River
LASHIO
Chindwin River
SHWEBO
BURMA ROAD.
ARAKAN
MANDALAY
MEIKTILA
Irrawaddy River

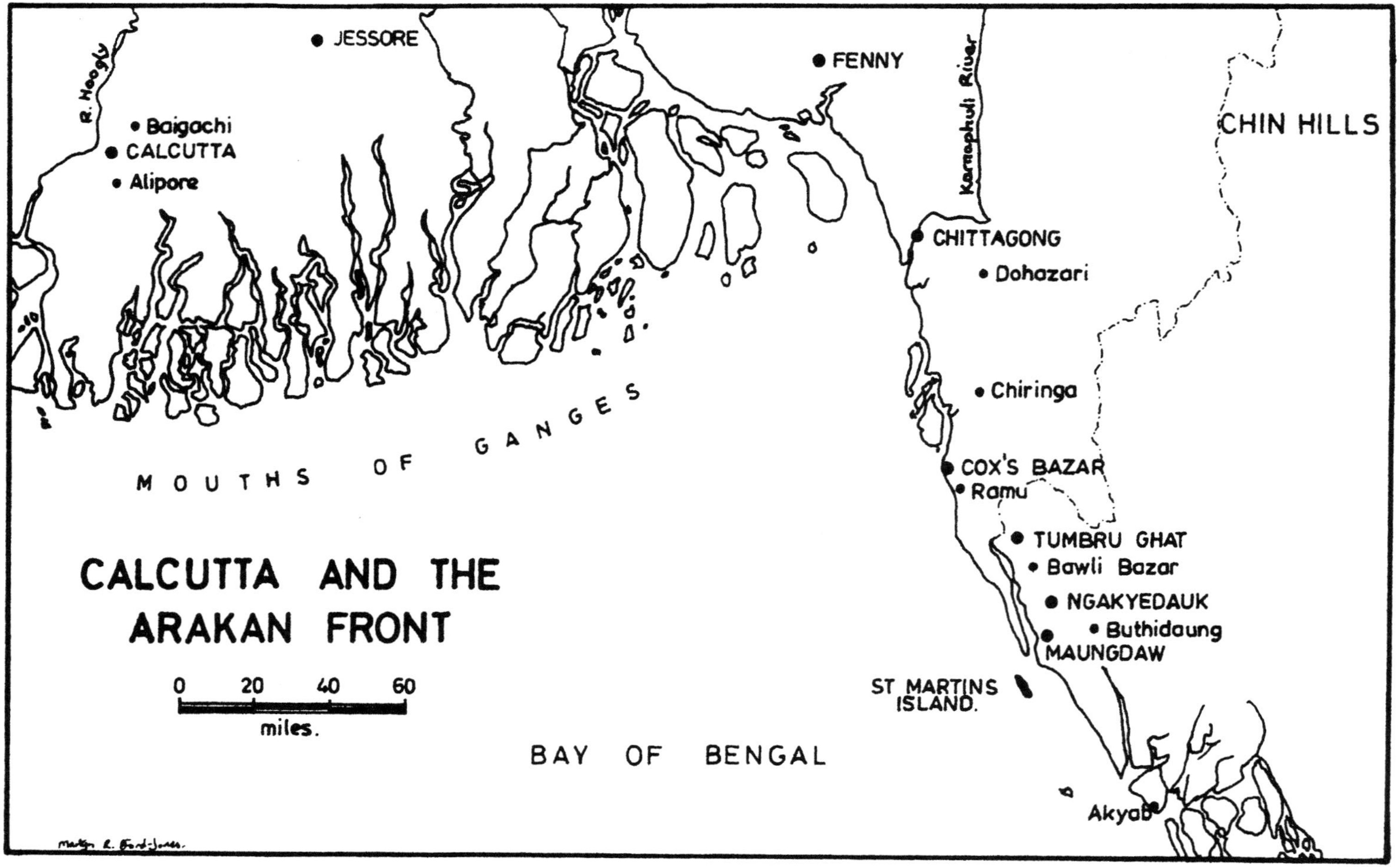
CALCUTTA AND THE
ARAKAN FRONT
0 20 40 60
miles.
R. Hoogly
JESSORE
Baigachi
CALCUTTA
Alipore
FENNY
Karnaphuli River
CHITTAGONG
Dohazari
Chiringa
COX'S BAZAR
Ramu
TUMBRU GHAT
Bawli Bazar
NGAKYEDAUK
Buthidaung
MAUNGDAW
ST MARTINS ISLAND.
Akyab
CHIN HILLS
MOUTHS OF GANGES
BAY OF BENGAL

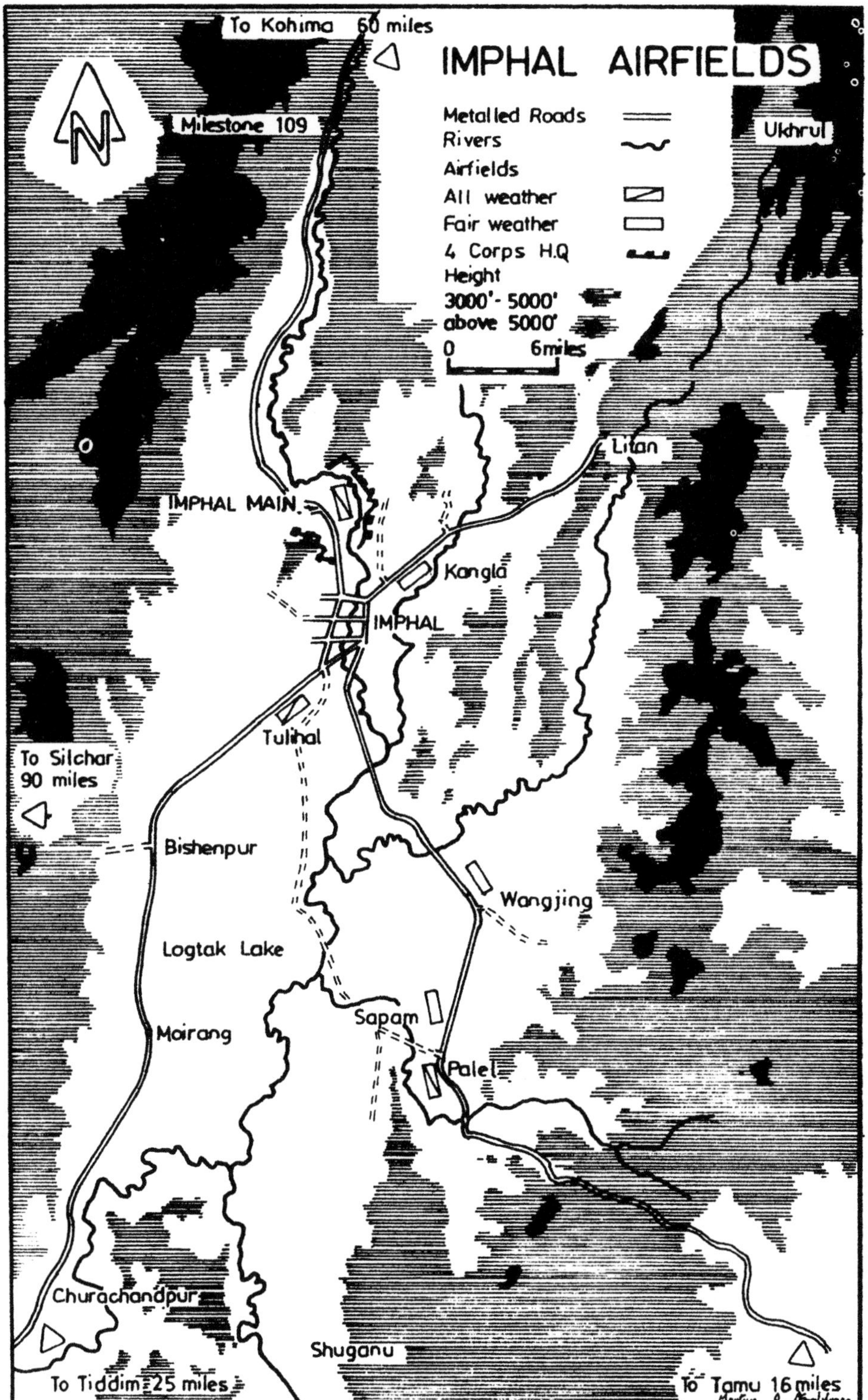
IMPHAL AIRFIELDS
Metalled Roads
Rivers
Airfields
All weather
Fair weather
4 Corps H.Q
Height
3000'- 5000'
above 5000'
0 6miles
To Kohima 60 miles
Milestone 109
Ukhrul
Litan
IMPHAL MAIN
Kangla
IMPHAL
Tulihal
To Silchar 90 miles
Bishenpur
Wangjing
Logtak Lake
Sapam
Moirang
Palel
Churachandpur
Shuganu
To Tiddim 25 miles
To Tamu 16 miles

Photographic Images

I have collected photographs connected with the RAF's war over Burma for more than thirty years, the vast majority of which have come from the personal collections of the pilots and ground crews involved in that conflict. As I have found with all my time writing to and interviewing these men (many of whom have died in the interim) and also those in European air battles, it is a fact that any number of them will have collected photos from each other. Long since forgotten is the name of the man who originally took the photograph, but several of his friends and colleagues will have asked for a copy for their own interest. Therefore to credit just the individual who gave me the picture to copy is often incorrect and, indeed, another former airman will have the same picture in his album. I have, therefore, listed below the names of those who provided the images and hope, in the interests of history, and with due reverence to the men who fought the Burma air war, that all will appreciate how difficult it is to know, with any degree of certainty, who the original picture taker was.

I. Adamson, D. J. Barnett, W. P. Bennett, J. M. Bott, D. Brocklehurst, K. Bunting, K. Clark, A. G. Conway, A. R. Corston, H. D. Costain, N. Cottrell, L. F. Cronin, I. D. Culpan, G. G. A. Davies, F. W. T. Davis, S. deHorne, Mr Denny, C. T. Doudy, H. J. Everard, G. Falconer, Mr Fox, R. E. Griffiths, W. A. Goold, J. P. Haley, P. W. Hall, L. C. C Hawkins, R. A. Hedderwick, K. Hemingway, G. J. C. Hogan, V. K. Jacobs, W. D. James, E. E. Kennington, J. Kemp, P. H. Lee, J. N. Mackenzie, C. P. N. Newman, D. B. F. Nicholls, A. McG. Peart, K. A. Perkin, B. Philpott, G. Pitchfork, A. Thomas, W. Turner, J. Ward, S. L. Weggery, F. E. Wilding, R. E. Windle.

Maps drawn by Martin Ford-Jones.

Bibliography

Hurricanes over Burma, by M. C. C. Cotton DFC. Titania Publishing Co., 1988

A Mouse in my Pocket, by Hedley J. Everard DFC. Valley Floatplane Services Ltd, 1988

Hurricanes over the Arakan by Norman Franks. Patrick Stephens Ltd, 1989

Spitfires over the Arakan, by Norman Franks. William Kimber & Co. Ltd., 1988

The Air Battle of Imphal, by Norman Franks. William Kimber & Co. Ltd., 1985

Frank 'Chota' Carey by Norman Franks, Grub Street, 2006

Wings over Burma, by K. Hemingway. Quality Press Ltd., 1944

The Woodpecker Story, by Sqn Ldr V. K. Jacobs. The Pentland Press, 1994

Bloody Shambles Vol 1, by Christopher F. Shores, *et al.* Grub Street, 1992

Bloody Shambles Vol 2, by Chistopher F. Shores, *et al.* Grub Street, 1992

Air War for Burma, by Christopher F. Shores. Grub Street, 2005